O. PEROVSKAYA

KIDS and CUBS

Fredonia Books
Amsterdam, The Netherlands

Kids and Cubs

by
Olga Perovskaya

ISBN: 1-58963-611-2

Copyright © 2001 by Fredonia Books

Reprinted from the 1981 edition

Fredonia Books
Amsterdam, the Netherlands
http://www.fredoniabooks.com

I dedicate these childhood recollections to the bright memory of my dear parents.

Olga Perovskaya

CONTENTS

DIANKA AND TOMCHIK

There is a fertile, blossoming plateau between two large rivers in Central Asia. Its name in Kazakh is Djety-Su, which means Seven Rivers. There are mountains, forests, green valleys and orchards in Seven Rivers. One city, especially, is famed for its great apple orchards. This is Alma-Ata, which means "Father of Apples".

The "Father of Apples" has become the capital of the rich Kazakh Republic, a great cultural and industrial centre, which the Turksib Railway connects with all the major cities of the Soviet Union. Trains from far-off Moscow pull in regularly at the magnificent Alma-Ata railway station.

The tall mansions of the various academies, institutes, theatres and cinemas sparkle in the sun like snow-white mountain caps, while the mountains tower majestically above the city.

Trams, trucks, trolley-buses and an endless stream of automobiles fill the broad streets and thorough-fares. Crowds of brightly dressed, sunburned tourists board sight-seeing buses to visit the parks and mountain resorts that surround the city.

This is how the once provincial, sleepy town of Alma-Ata has changed. It is no longer as I knew it in the far-off days of my childhood.

When I was a child, Alma-Ata was 400 miles from the nearest railway. Its population was very small, and if a single automobile appeared on the streets in the course of a year, everyone within running distance would leave whatever they were doing and dash out to see the miracle on wheels.

In those days all the houses were one-storied. They looked like little mushrooms peeping out from among branching trees.

We lived in a little house with a large orchard. There were many apple-trees, but, more important still, there were many pets, both farm and wild animals, that were growing up together with us.

Every time my father went hunting he would bring back live baby animals. We fed them, took care of them and brought them up ourselves.

Each of us had our own special pet — one had a lively fox-cub, another a baby donkey and my youngest sister had a guinea-pig.

"I'll bring you back a wolf-cub," Father promised me.

"A wo-o-lf? Oh, no! That's too scary. It's too hard to tame a wolf. Bring me something else instead, won't you?"

"I hope you're not serious," Mother said. "It'll bite the children and scratch them and run away."

"Oh, you scaredy-cats! Are you really frightened of a tiny baby cub? Too bad, because wolves can become wonderfully tame."

And he told us the true story of a tame wolf.

The wolf loved its master like the most devoted of dogs. It followed him everywhere, it protected him from his enemies and guarded his horse whenever they went on trips. Its only shortcoming was that it liked to drink. As soon as the wolf smelled liquor, it would go sniffing about the house until it finally found the bottle. Then it would roll it about the floor until it broke and it would lap up the vodka.

"After the wolf drank all the vodka did it become as noisy as Timka Frolov?" we asked. "Did it break dishes and fight?"

"No, it never did anything like that. It would just crawl into a corner and go to sleep."

"And then what?"

"And then, when it woke up, it would be just as clever and hard-working as before."

"That's not what I meant. What happened afterwards?"

"Afterwards? Well, its master had to go far away travelling by coach and train. The man didn't know what things would be like in his new place of work, or whether they would want to take him on with a wolf. So he decided to give the wolf to his friends. But the wolf didn't want to live with them. Then the man took it to a forest. But the wolf found its way back and got home before the man did. Finally, there was nothing to be done except put it to sleep. The man gave it some medicine and the wolf collapsed. Its master was terribly grieved. He got into a carriage and set out. After travelling for some time he noticed that his wolf was loping along after the carriage. The dose of medicine had been too small. The wolf soon revived and dashed after its master. From then on the wolf travelled in the carriage with him for nearly five hundred miles to the nearest railroad. Then they went by train and by boat. The man said the wolf was his dog, and it behaved so well that no one ever doubted his word. The wolf lived to a ripe old age and they never parted again."

"How wonderful!" we all said. "Now tell us another story about wolves."

"What's the use of telling you stories? I'll bring you back a live wolf-cub and you can take care of it yourselves. Then you'll be able to tell me interesting things, not the other way round."

From then on I would nag my father every single day:

"Where's my wolf-cub? You promised me one. Where is it?"

And then one morning when I was still asleep someone came over to my bed and said in a very loud voice:

"Get up! They've brought him!"

I knew exactly what it was. I jumped out of bed, pulled on my clothes and dashed out into the yard.

"Run to the smithy!" Father shouted after me. There was a deserted smithy in a far corner of the yard where all kind of junk, like rusty iron, broken sledges and broken dishes, was dumped. The door to the smithy was tightly closed and a big stone was placed against it. I pulled the door open a crack and squeezed in. It was dark inside. Coming in from the bright sunshine I couldn't make anything out.

Suddenly I heard a rustling sound from under the hearth, where the blacksmiths make their fire. Four bright-green eyes shone in the dark. I shuddered and tried to back away. I didn't think I would ever be afraid of a little wolf-cub, but this one ... this one had four eyes!

"Silly! There are two of them."

The cubs growled. Judging by the noise they made, they were creeping farther under the stove.

I already knew that the best way to make friends with an animal is to give it something to eat. I ran back to the kitchen, filled a bowl with milk, soaked some

13

bread in it and took it to the smithy. I left the door ajar so that some light would enter. Then I set the bowl on the earthen floor and hid in the darkness.

The cubs were afraid to come close to the food. A long time passed. But they were hungry and it did smell delicious.

Finally, a tiny grey muzzle peeped out. It was immediately joined by another. The cubs crawled out, looked around and crept cautiously towards the bowl.

Here they forgot their fear. Standing with their paws spread far apart they fished out chunks of bread, shivered, choked and jostled each other. Since they had to swallow and growl at the same time, they kept choking and coughing right into the bowl, making the milk bubble.

They were so busy eating they did not notice me. I tiptoed up very close.

The cubs were just like puppies, they had large round bellies and large paws. The only difference was that their tails were thinner and not as furry and their ears were stiff and pointed.

Soon there was nothing left in the bowl, but the cubs were not through with it yet. One had all four feet in it and was licking it clean. The other raised its head, started and stared at me. I saw that it was confused, so I smiled and put my hand out to pat it.

Snap!

I barely had time to pull my hand away. The cub darted back.

What a mean thing he was! Though still a baby, he wouldn't let anyone pat him. Why, he nearly bit my finger off! And what had I done? I had given him some bread and milk. Well, I'd show him!

I didn't try to force my friendship on the cubs, but to tell the truth I felt hurt.

The children surrounded me when I came out into the yard.

"Did you see the wolves? What are they like?"

"They're excellent wolves," I replied without batting an eye. "They're nearly used to me already

15

and they obey me. Now I have to think of names for them."

We sat down on some logs nearby and began to think. Father had said that one was a male and one was a female, and so we named them Tomchik and Dianka.

At noon I brought them some more food and called to them, making little clucking sounds.

The cubs crawled out and began to eat. I opened the door wide. Our dogs looked into the smithy. I was afraid they would attack the cubs and wanted to chase them away, but the cubs ran to them with their tails between their legs and big smiles on their faces. They tried to lick the dogs' noses, they rolled over on their backs and kicked their feet in the air and played up to them just like real puppies would. They probably thought the dogs were wolves, and that is why they were so happy.

The dogs growled. They were much more interested in the bowl of food than in the two little cubs. They sniffed at the bowl, finished off whatever was left and went out again.

The cubs were so happy to have found the dogs that they forgot their fear and caution and scrambled after them. They were quite far from the smithy when they suddenly looked around in terror. The yard didn't look at all like the forest.

They saw a wagon and crouched low, curling back their lips. They waited a bit, but the wagon did not move. It didn't look as if it were getting ready to attack them. Now they felt braver.

Stretching their necks and still trembling, they finally reached the middle of the yard.

The dogs had long since run off to the porch, leaving the cubs all alone. They whined pitifully, but the dogs had no intention of coming back. Then the cubs started off again.

As luck would have it, they had to pass the barn. Our dog Lute and her new-born puppies lived under the barn. Lute decided that the cubs were after her puppies and came flying out at them. She grabbed Tomchik by the scruff of his neck and shook him angrily. We came running to the rescue.

Lute let him go. Then both he and Dianka ran off to the smithy, crawled far under the stove and were quiet.

Poor Tomchik! Look what had happened to him on his very first outing!

We crowded round the smithy guiltily, peering under the stove, calling gently to the cubs and pushing all sorts of tasty titbits towards them. They were good enough to eat our offerings, but their only response was an angry growling.

However, no matter how hurt their feelings were, they couldn't stay under the stove long. Dianka was the first to stick her head out. She crawled out, sat outside for a while and then darted under the stove again.

Then Tomchik came out. There was blood on his ear, the fur on his head was all ruffled and there was a scratch under his eye. He kept shaking his head and bending his sore ear towards the ground. There they sat, side by side on the threshold of the smithy, looking out into the yard, feeling hurt and lonely.

The next day passed in the same way. But when I came to feed them on the third morning, they were standing by the door, waiting.

We noticed that Dianka was much bolder than her brother. She was the first to come out when we called, and at the sight of the bowl she would begin to lick her chops anxiously.

Dianka followed me into the yard. Without realising what she was doing, she crawled up the porch steps after me. Tomchik remained below.

We were having tea on the porch. Everyone smiled at Dianka and treated her to something tasty. Feeling quite content after having had her fill of tasty morsels, she went down to her brother.

The coward Tomchik sniffed at her muzzle and realised that she had had something good to eat. He licked his chops and sniffed at her again, while she stood there happily. Her eyes shone like beads, her belly was so full that her tail stuck up in the air and would not go down. She seemed to be saying: see how nice it is to be brave!

Then they both set out to have a look around. This time they didn't look as frightened as before. They walked about the yard, rounded the house and found themselves in the orchard.

I followed quietly behind. The orchard must have reminded them of the forest, for they seemed to have grown taller with their new-found confidence, they became bolder and made a dash for the bushes. Then they ran out into the clearing, played for a while and disappeared among the trees again. They sniffed at every tree and bush. Finally, when they were all worn out, they fell asleep in a cherry thicket. I left them there. Later on I brought their dinner to them there, but they were gone. I called them again and again, peering into the distance, trying to see if they were coming.

Finally, I set the bowl on the grass and sat down next to it, mixing the food with a twig.

Where could they be?

I was beginning to worry. Suddenly I saw two muzzles in the bushes next to me! They had probably crept up long ago and were watching my every move. Perhaps they thought I was blind not to have noticed them right under my very nose.

But how could I have noticed them? Even though they were fat and clumsy, they made less noise than a butterfly.

While they were eating I stretched out on the grass and made believe I was asleep. Perhaps it was the

orchard and their feeling of freedom, or perhaps they
were simply getting used to me. However it was, they
behaved very rudely: one cub breathed right in my
face, while the other tugged at my dress and my braid.
Dianka stole my shoe and dragged it off into the
bushes. Tomchik ran to get it from her. When I finally
took their new toy away it was in a very sad condition.

They spent the whole day in the orchard and
remained there for the night.

Several days passed. The cubs had complete
freedom. My only worry was to keep them well fed,
so that they would not take it into their heads to go
hunting on their own.

Their first feeding was at dawn, which was about 5
a.m. Since I didn't want to wake anyone, I prepared

their food in the evening and kept it near my bed. At sunrise I would climb through my window into the orchard, find the cubs and feed them. After they had eaten, I would take the bowl, climb back through my window, tumble into bed and fall sound asleep.

The cubs would see me off as far as the window. If I ever overslept they would come to my window, get up on their hind legs, raise their heads and howl.

My bed was right by the window. I would stick my head out and as soon as they saw that I was awake they would begin to jump with joy.

Soon they became quite tame. I was very attached to them, and if I did not see them for several hours, I would really begin to miss them.

I spent long hours playing with the cubs. We rolled in the grass and ran about the orchard. Whenever I came there to read they would hunt me out immediately, sit down facing me and after waiting a few minutes would begin to tease.

Once Dianka became very bored with my reading. She yawned loudly and sat down on my book. I shoved her off, rolled her over and dragged her through the grass by her hind paws. Meanwhile, however, Tomchik had grabbed my book and was tearing it to bits with the greatest of pleasure.

The cubs had a funny habit. After they had eaten, their bellies would blow up and become very firm. Then they would lie down and crawl about, rubbing their tummies on the grass.

It was really amazing: even though they knew nothing about medicine, they understood that massage was a very good thing.

Once, when I was wandering about the orchard, I decided to have some plums. Since I could not reach them from below, I climbed a tree and began shaking the branches. The ripe plums fell to the ground with loud plops. I knew I had shaken quite a few plums off, but when I came down I couldn't find any. How strange, I thought. Back up I went again and shook the branches. When I climbed down I saw that Dianka and Tomchik were gobbling up all my plums!

That is how I discovered that they loved fruit and knew what was tasty, for they always ate the ripest pieces. After that I often treated them, shaking the branches of the plum, apricot and apple-trees.

Dianka and Tomchik knew every nook and cranny of the orchard, but they rarely came up to the house, because they didn't like company. I was the only human being they accepted and loved. They would come to greet me, nuzzle close to me, jump up and put their paws on my shoulders and lick my hands and face.

Once I boasted that the cubs knew my voice and could recognise it from among all others.

Everyone made fun of me.

"That's not true. They can't recognise your voice at all. They just come to be fed. It doesn't matter who feeds you if you're really hungry."

"Yes, it does," I insisted. "Let's try and see."

About eight children came to watch the experiment. Even the grown-ups were interested.

Everyone crowded round the orchard gate.

"Wait! Give me the bowl of food," my sister said.

She took the bowl, went into the orchard and began calling the cubs. But no matter how long she called them no one came out. She returned in disgrace.

Then another child tried his luck, and a third. Everyone had a turn. Finally, I said:

"I don't even need the bowl. They'll come to me anyway."

To tell the truth, I wasn't as sure as I sounded. What if they didn't come after all?

"Dianka! Tomchik!" I called, and all the while my heart was beating wildly.

Then everyone saw them running towards me. They came immediately, they had been waiting for me to call them.

"See! And you said they couldn't recognise my voice!"

The summer was coming to an end. The cubs had grown considerably, and the dogs had become very respectful. When Dianka and Tomchik had been very small the dogs had paid no attention to them. But things had changed now, and they would often come to visit my pets.

One day the dogs came running into the orchard.
They raced round the trees, barked, yelped with
pleasure and tumbled about. It was a dazzlingly bright
morning. The ground was soft, and the fallen leaves
were so tempting the dogs just had to bury their noses
in them. They tossed up piles of leaves and seemed
unable to stop even for a moment. It was as if
someone had wound them up and now the springs
were making them go. The cubs were excited by the
dogs and soon joined the game. Dianka smacked
Tomchik sharply with her paw, darted away,

crouched and waited, as if to say: "Come on, Tomchik! Let's show them how wolves play!"

Then pandemonium broke loose. In no time Dianka was racing away from Zagrai, while Lute was pulling Tomchik's tail. When he whirled around and knocked her over she was not at all offended. She jumped up, shook herself and continued the game with even more spirit than before.

From then on the dogs came to the orchard every day. Dianka and Tomchik would sometimes follow them back into the yard. The dogs and the wolves became real friends.

This is very rare, but once a wolf has made a dog its friend, it is a lasting friendship.

I will tell you the true story of a Yakut in the North and his dog.

The man had camped with his reindeer. It was winter. There was not a single house or dog for miles around. He had a dog, a husky, which watched his herd. Then the man began to notice that the dog was carrying dried fish off to the forest. He followed the dog but could not discover anything. Each day the dog carried off some fish. "Why doesn't she eat it herself? Where is she taking it?" he wondered. That spring the dog unexpectedly had a litter of puppies. The man was very pleased, for puppies are always welcome in the household of a Yakut reindeer-breeder. You can get a reindeer for a good dog in the North. He could see that these puppies were really fine. They were strong and sturdy and kept growing by leaps and bounds. Soon the man was ready to move to his summer pasture. He packed his belongings, piled everything on his sledge and set out, with the dog and the half-grown puppies trotting behind. Their way lay through the forest. Suddenly the man turned around and saw that a wolf had joined his dog family. He grabbed up his gun and was about to shoot it when a sudden thought came to him. He realised that the wolf had fathered the litter of puppies and that his dog had been stealing dried fish for it all winter. He put down his gun and the wolf followed them to the summer pasture.

Dianka and Tomchik were nearly full-grown by winter. Their fur was thick and long and they had sideburns on their jowls. Their tails became furry and soft. Now they were as big as large, powerful dogs.

Not long before the first snow fell they made themselves a den. It was so big that the dogs would sometimes crawl into it to sleep with the wolves.

This friendship with the dogs had a bad effect on the wolves, for the dogs had taught them to steal chickens. Since they were always punished for this at home, they would jump over the fence and catch our neighbour's chickens. One day the neighbour came to see my father. He was carrying a dead turkey and said that our cubs had killed it. He wanted us to pay for it.

"And I'm warning you," he said as he left, "if I ever see them in my yard again, you'll be sorry."

That very day Dianka and Tomchik were put on chains. Life no longer was as free and easy as it had been.

One morning an organ-grinder came into our yard and began playing a waltz. Suddenly, a strange hoarse voice joined in from behind the barn and then a second joined the first. Our wolves were singing with the organ-grinder. No sooner had they begun than the dogs crawled out from everywhere. They, too, raised their heads and howled in every key. This concert made the organ-grinder laugh so hard that tears streamed down his cheeks. He paid no more attention to what he was playing, and no one could hear the music anyway, but he kept on turning the handle for the shaggy chorus.

The cubs often howled, for it was no fun for freedom-loving creatures to be chained and imprisoned. As soon as twilight settled on the town they would begin their mournful howling.

We noticed that the dogs had learned to howl like wolves and that the wolves had learned to bark like dogs.

At first, Father would not believe this was true, but I soon convinced him. Once, when Dianka was barking, I went to call my father. He was very surprised and said this was very rare.

In order to cheer up the wolves we would take them

for walks on leashes to the field beyond town. Whenever we had a free moment we would all set off. The wolves trotted along nicely, but we were very bad companions for them on these walks. We would soon be so tired we could hardly see straight, while they would just be getting into the swing of it.

They were restless because they were not getting enough exercise, and they tried to break their chains. Finally, they learned how to free themselves. They would somehow press the spring of the latch and would take the chains off their collars. Whenever they got loose everyone would come running for me, for they obeyed only me.

Every now and then someone would say:

"Come on, Wolf-Sister (that is what they called me). Go tie up your beauties!"

Just before New Year's, someone shouted:

"Tomchik is loose and he's in the neighbour's yard!"

I ran out of the house without bothering to put on my hat or coat and took the short cut through the orchard. There were no paths in the orchard in winter, and the snow was knee-high.

I could see through the fence: there was Tomchik, standing in the middle of the yard; the neighbour had come out of the house carrying his gun.

"Wait!" I screamed from afar. "Wait! I'm coming! I'll tie him up! Don't sh..." My voice faltered as I saw the neighbour raise his gun and shoot. Tomchik fell lifeless to the ground.

I ran over to him, flung the chain at the neighbour, grabbed hold of his coat and shook it, repeating over and over again:

"Look what you've done! Look what you've done!"

A crowd had gathered. Everyone was talking at once.

I put Tomchik's lifeless head on my lap and wept bitterly as I sat there in the snow. I do not recall coming home, or how Tomchik was brought home.

By evening I was gravely ill and had a very high fever.

I spent the next two months in bed.

Dianka was now all alone. Tomchik was gone, I was sick, and she was terribly unhappy. The first days after Tomchik's death she would not even eat. She howled, paced up and down, and everyone thought she would die.

During my illness I was delirious. Whenever my head cleared I would beg everyone to be good to Dianka, to feed her and take good care of her.

"Did you feed Dianka? Is Dianka sleeping?" I would ask whenever they brought me broth or medicine.

"Dianka's a good sport! She's been eating like a wolf and she's probably forgotten Tomchik already."

As soon as I was feeling a little better, I asked them to bring her to me. A huge she-wolf entered the room, dragging her chain. At first, I didn't even recognise her. She looked very menacing. She did not recognise me, either, although I did not look menacing at all: my hair had been bobbed, and I was now terribly thin.

Dianka sniffed at everything curiously. I called to her:

"Dianka! Dianka!"

She recognised my voice immediately and ran up to me. As I patted her she closed her eyes with pleasure and stood wagging her tail.

A fat tomcat was sitting on my bed. He did not like Dianka. He decided it was just another nosey dog, and he was used to having his way with dogs.

He began to hiss and smacked Dianka sharply on the muzzle! I caught my breath.

The fur rose on Dianka's back. She opened up her terrible jaws and....

"Dianka! Dearie! Sweetie!"

I threw myself on her neck. She picked the cat up and, holding it gingerly by the back, carried it off the bed, set it on the floor and returned to me.

Every spring we moved to a cottage in the woods, ten miles from town. The cottage was in the mountains, near a stream. There were many flowers in the meadows and higher up, near the snow caps, were the summer camps of the Kazakh shepherds. Their children were our best friends. We loved our summer cottage and were always happy when we moved in spring.

That year I was terribly anxious to move, for I thought that Dianka would not have to be tied up in the mountains.

But I was wrong, for there was a village nearby, and the people were afraid of a wolf wandering about.

One day Dianka broke loose and headed for the village. A vicious mongrel ran out and attacked Dianka in a rage. It was a fearless dog, indeed! Dianka snapped at it. The next moment the dog was dead. Some people came running out of the house carrying sticks and whips. When Dianka saw that things were going badly she hid behind me, peeping out mischievously, as if to say: "I'm safe here, no one can touch me now!"

And sure enough, I would not let them harm her. But they shouted and scolded and went off to complain to my parents.

Several months passed. Would Dianka have to spend her whole life chained up? Father tried to coax me into letting her free, but it took me a long time to agree.

"If you were chained up you'd know what it was like," he said. So I decided to try it out. I sat down next to Dianka and spent the whole day with her. Then I agreed with Father. One morning I gave her a very big breakfast. Father saddled his horse, took up the end of her chain, and Dianka trotted happily after him.

He took her farther into the forest and removed her collar. She was gone in a flash.

"It's true," my father thought, "no matter how well you feed a wolf, it will always have one eye on the forest."

He waited until Dianka was gone and then set out for home. He did not return until evening.

"Is she gone?"

"Yes. She even forgot to send her regards."

"Well, I don't care. I'm glad," I said. I hung my head, for it was sad to think that my friend had left me so easily.

Just then something cold touched my hand. I turned around. It was Dianka! She had followed my father back home.

We tried to make her go another time. Father took her far into the forest. Then he set off in a direction opposite to our house and crossed a mountain pass.

Four days passed. Dianka returned again, tired, hungry and full of burrs. You could see that she had been lost but she had found her way home at last.

I don't know how this all would have ended if we had not moved to another town. We were faced with a problem of what to do with our pets.

Naturally, I was most concerned about Dianka. I kept thinking of the story my father had told us about the wolf whose master had tried to put it to sleep. I did my best to arrange for a new home for her where she would be as happy as she had been with us.

And then, quite unexpectedly, everything turned out much better than we had ever hoped for.

There had been several robberies in our town and in the surrounding villages in the past six months. The thieves had got away with horses and cows and no one knew what they had done with them. Several excellent police dogs were brought in. A detective arrived with the dogs and he was put in charge of the case.

My father and I saw the dogs. They had a big yard to themselves with lots of trees. Each dog had its own kennel. They were well fed and no one was allowed to abuse them.

These dogs looked so very much like wolves that I was immediately struck by an idea: could I ask them to take Dianka? I told Father about my idea and he spoke with the man in charge.

"A she-wolf? A tame one?" the man shouted excitedly. "Why, that's the dream of my life! Bring her right over. That's just what I've been looking for!"

And so Dianka moved to the kennels and now shared one with a police dog by the name of Wolf.

I spent every day before we left visiting her. She always met me lovingly. She looked well-fed, happy and content, and so when we left my mind was at ease, for I knew she would be well cared for.

We had no pets in our new home and we missed our old ones. I always tried to discover what I could of Dianka. For two or three years the man in charge of the kennels wrote to us often. He said that Dianka had had puppies, that they were unusually sturdy and healthy and, what was most important, that they had turned out to be excellent police dogs.

After a while he stopped writing. It was not until many years later that we learned that the kennels had become famous throughout Kazakhstan. Its dogs would always find their criminals. No one could hide from them. In fact, thieves were so frightened of these dogs that crime had practically been wiped out in Alma-Ata.

Several years later we returned to Alma-Ata. The first thing I did was to go to the kennels. One of the attendants said that Dianka and Wolf had both died of old age.

"But what about their puppies?" I asked. "Are there any left?"

"All the dogs are at the hippodrome now. There's a kennel show and contest today."

I rushed to the hippodrome. The stands were as crowded as on the days of the major races.

It was fascinating. First the young dogs who had just begun training were paraded. They went through their paces diligently, jumping over obstacles, climbing up ladders and carrying bags of ammunition across the field. They had to find things that had been hidden and carry out other orders.

Suddenly, the box-office cashier came running up, shouting that he had been held up and robbed. The crowd became excited. People looked into their pockets to see if their own money was safe.

A dog was immediately put on the trail of the thieves. It sniffed the box-office and made a dash for the stands, running past the first three rows. A well-dressed woman was sitting in the middle of the fourth row. She was wearing one of the tremendous hats that were stylish at the time.

The dog ran up to the woman, sniffed at her and put its paws on her shoulders! The woman tried to push the dog away.

"What's the meaning of this?" she cried indignantly in a funny, squeaky voice. "This is outrageous! I'll complain to the management!"

"How terrible," the people in the crowd agreed. "Does such a woman look like a thief? Why, she's been here from the very start."

"The dog's made a mistake. Where are the attendants? Why doesn't someone take it away?"

"Why, a crazy dog like that might bite any innocent bystander!"

But the dog did not understand what the people were saying and went about its business. It sunk its teeth into the stylish hat and yanked it off together with the woman's hair.

"Help! Look what it's doing!" the woman standing next to me screamed.

"This is horrible!" another woman gasped.

But suddenly we all saw a head with cropped hair appear from under the woman's large hat and long hair. Then we looked at the dog. It was tearing the hat and wig apart. Then it pulled out a large packet of bills that had been carefully tied together. It held the packet in its mouth as it stared at the woman.

Now the woman began pulling her dress over her head in full view of the crowd. She had on a uniform and knee boots underneath.

"Why, it's one of the attendants!" somebody said.

Everyone laughed and clapped. They all wanted to pat the intelligent dog, but the man said that strangers were not allowed to pat service dogs.

There were several other skits on the programme where the dogs again demonstrated their perfect training, their intelligence, courage and wonderful sense of smell.

Then there was a parade of dogs.

In conclusion, the best dogs were trotted out, their names were announced, their accomplishments listed and prizes were awarded, while the band played a fanfare for each prize.

"Joy and Spy!" the master of ceremonies announced in a triumphant voice. "The offspring of Wolf and Dianka, a pure-bred wolf. They have just returned from Moscow where they won the Grand Prize and gold medal. These dogs are not taking part in the present competition, because no other dog here can compete with them."

Everyone clapped and people stood up to get a

better look at the famous pair. The band played another fanfare. Two great and beautiful wolves stood before us. I admired them as I recalled our own Dianka and Tomchik.

MISHKA

Everyone was asleep in the little cottage. The river roared at the foot of the mountain, rolling along the heavy stones. Suddenly, we heard the sound of men shouting.

"Giddy-up! Come on, Gnedoi!" A heavily laden wagon rolled up the steep road and stopped outside the gate.

The horses lowered their heads and breathed heavily.

Father walked around the house to see if anyone was up and then knocked at the window with the handle of his whip.

"I'm coming!" Mother called from within.

While she was dressing, Father and his friend, Fedot Ivanovich, were busy untying something that was stretched out on the wagon. They placed it on the ground carefully and undid the ropes around it.

Gnedoi, happy to be home at last, kept nudging the locked gate with his nose. The gate finally opened, the wagon rolled into the yard and stopped near the barn.

"What took you so long?" Mother asked as she helped unload the packages. "I was beginning to worry."

"We ran into a little unexpected business. It put us off but it certainly was worth it. Look what we've brought! It's a present for the girls."

And he pointed to something that looked like a calf in the darkness.

"Goodness! Where did you find it? How did such a baby manage to survive? Come, bring him into the barn. Perhaps I'd better feed him. Is he hungry?"

"No, he won't eat now. He's too shaken up from the journey. Let him rest. We'll give him some milk in the morning."

Father bedded the "present" down on some straw, tucked a horse blanket around it, shut the barn door and rolled a heavy stone against it.

"Where do you think you're going? Go on, stupid!" he shouted at the shaggy mongrel, Mailik.

Mailik was having a hard time trying to attract his master's attention. As soon as he had heard voices at the foot of the hill he had raced down to greet them. He had licked the horses' muzzles and his master's boots and spun around the yard like a top, wagging his tail for all he was worth. He was doing his best to express his joy and love for the late arrival. And when Father rolled the stone over against the barn door, Mailik got his front paws around it and tried to roll it back to where it had been.

"He's gone crazy from joy," Father laughed. "Maybe he wants to get into the barn. He might kill the baby by accident."

"I don't think he wants to get in. He's just trying to help you and earn some praise. Go on, Mailik! Don't make a nuisance of yourself."

My sister Sonya and I had been awakened by the noise. We took a pail and ran for water for tea.

Soon the samovar was hissing on the porch. Mother was frying pancakes. As we sat around the table drinking tea Father told us about our "present". It had been left all alone in the forest beside its dead mother, who had been killed by a treacherous hunter.

"What terrible people there are! They know that animals have babies in the spring and that you're not allowed to hunt them. But still they keep on shooting. They killed his mother and there he was, nuzzling close to her. And what else could he do, such a tiny little thing? We didn't have the heart to kill him, so we decided to take him along. He can grow up here with the children."

41

Mother was all in favour of the idea.

She had taken a liking to the little "present" from the very first and now became his true defender.

Yulia and Natasha finally woke up. They had heard Father and Mother talking about a present and stuck their sleepy heads in the door.

"Mamma, can we eat the present?" Natasha asked in a deep, husky voice.

"No," Yulia said, "it's alive."

"Mamma, what is it?"

"Mamma, is it for us? Where is it? Can we see it, Mamma?"

"Off to bed with you!" Mother scolded. "You'll see him in the morning."

There was nothing they could do. They would just have to wait till morning.

Mother awoke at the crack of dawn. She got up and awakened Sonya and me, and the three of us went out into the yard. The horses had not yet been fed. They had cooled off during the night and were hungry. When they saw us, they whinnied softly.

We took off their harnesses and led them down to the river. There they drank their fill, trotted back to the yard and headed straight for the trough, where they munched the sweet clover.

Sonya milked the cow and let it out to pasture. The cow set off by itself for a meadow in the mountains.

Mother went into the house, poured some fresh milk into a little pail and called to our younger sisters.

"Come on, sleepy-heads! Get up! We're going to feed our little guest."

Yulia jumped to her feet, put on her dress and sandals and ran after Mother. She was trembling more from excitement than from the morning chill.

The barn door was wide open and we could hear Sonya saying gently:

"Come on, silly, don't be afraid."

A tiny deer was standing in the straw next to her, sucking her fingers.

Yulia was speechless with joy.

She sat down next to the baby and began patting its head and its legs, gazing into its eyes and chattering excitedly all the while.

"Why are his legs so thin? How old is he? Where are his Mamma and Papa? Did he come in the wagon? Look! He licked my hand!" And she laughed happily. "That means he's hungry.'

Mother put her finger in his mouth and pulled his head gently down into the little pail. The baby deer understood what it was and began sucking her finger loudly and with it the milk from the pail.

He swallowed greedily and choked and coughed when the milk got into his nose. We watched him and whispered about his every movement:

"Look how wide he spread his legs."

"That's to keep from falling."

"But see how shaky they are, anyway. They look as though they'll break any minute."

43

"No, he's spread them apart like that to make more room in his stomach."

"See him push the pail! Just like a calf that's nursing."

"What does he think it is, a cow? Isn't he silly!"

Yulia and I shook with laughter. Sonya looked at us sternly and said:

"You must think you're terribly smart! Why, you don't even know what he is."

"Yes, we do! He's a baby deer."

"You're baby deer yourselves! He's a Siberian stag, that's what! He's called a maral. I know all about marals, 'cause I read about them in Brehm's *Animal World.*"

We could not match her knowledge and said no more, but looked at the "maral" with new respect. He had long thin legs and sharp hoofs, a skinny neck and a broad round head with large floppy ears which kept twitching constantly. His eyes were like large plums. His forehead was broad, his nose was small and his nostrils were dilated. He was as tall as a new-born colt.

There were white spots on his soft furry sides, and my hand itched to pat him. He had no tail to speak of, just a tiny little stub with a white spot around it, as if someone had spread a white napkin around his tail.

"What's his name, Mamma?"

"We've named him Mishka, because he was found near the village of Mikhailovka," Sonya said haughtily. "That's what we named him last night when you were all sleeping."

It was simply amazing, the way she liked to brag about her knowledge. No sooner had she passed on this bit of information than she began to tell us all about Mishka, as if it were she who had found him and brought him home.

Meanwhile, Mishka had finished his milk. He tilted the pail and licked up the last drops. Then he began wagging his stubby tail and butting the pail.

The pail rolled out into the yard. Mishka followed it. He stuck his head into it again and began pushing it about.

He was hoping that the pail, like a mother deer, would give him some more milk if he butted it hard enough.

Little Natasha came out on the porch. She had just got up and looked about crossly.

Mishka was still clattering around with his head inside the pail.

Suddenly, he jerked his head back and leaped sideways with all four legs off the ground. Then he looked around, edged over to Mailik in little hops, lowered his head and began jumping and kicking out in all directions.

Mailik stood up and opened his eyes wide in surprise as he watched the dancer. He growled loudly. Mishka sprang upwards like a rocket. He raced over to Mother, hid behind her and then stuck his head out to have a cautious look at Mailik. Then he squeaked, making a funny *eek-eek-eek* sound.

His nostrils were dilated, his ears stood up in sharp points and his sides heaved in and out as he breathed heavily from fright.

Natasha laughed in her deep voice and jumped up and down with glee.

"He sounds just like a cat. And Mailik showed him, didn't he!"

When the samovar came to a boil and we all went into the house, Mishka clambered up the porch steps after us. While we were having our tea he clattered about the room, sniffing at everything. He stuck his nose out of the window, under the bed and into the earthenware jugs on the bench. Then he went to investigate the next room. He finally found a comfortable place (right on the threshold, in everyone's way), went down on his knees and then lay down.

There was a piece of paper on the floor next to him. Mishka picked it up with his lips. It rustled loudly as he began to chew it.

Four-year-old Natasha watched him eat the paper intently. Then she climbed off her chair, took a chunk of bread and began pulling out the soft part. Sonya nudged me. Yulia picked up the newspaper and hid her head behind it, shaking with laughter.

"What are you doing?" Mother asked.

46

"He's hungry," Natasha said gloomily. "See, he's even eating paper."

"No, he's not. He's just munching on it. We've already fed him. He's not a bit hungry."

"Yes, he is! If he's eating paper, it means he's hungry!"

She sat down next to Mishka and offered him the crust. He swallowed the paper, then accepted the crust and began champing it so greedily, one would think he hadn't had a thing to eat for the past three days.

Natasha beamed.

"See him eat it? And you said he wasn't hungry."

After breakfast we went out to play in the meadow, but Mishka stayed behind with Mother, following her like a shadow the whole day long, from the closet to the barn, from the barn to the brick stove in the far corner of the yard. While Mother cooked our lunch he lay quietly next to her, flicking his ears from time to time. Mishka did not like to be left alone in the yard, for he found it both frightening and lonely. Every time he crossed the yard after Mother he bumped into Mailik. He would shake his head at the dog and stamp a hoof angrily, as if trying to show Mailik that he had not forgotten the morning's quarrel.

And each time Mailik answered with a loud growl.

By noon Mishka was very hungry again. He kept getting in Mother's way, butting her impatiently in the stomach, as if saying: "Where's my milk?"

47

Mishka seemed to think that she was his mother and that it was her duty to feed him.

Mother laughed and tried to push him away as she got his dinner ready. When she set the pail of milk on the ground Mishka knew exactly what to do. He did not need her finger to guide him this time. He stuck his head in the pail and began drinking. But he was in such a hurry and so greedy that he knocked the pail over, spilling the milk.

"Oh, dear!" Mother said angrily. "I've done my best to please him and he went and knocked over the pail."

But no matter how she grumbled, she had to give him some more milk, for he was getting ready to butt her again, so there was nothing she could do but fill up the pail once more.

During the first few days Mishka tagged along after Mother. He spent a lot of time eating and sleeping and paid no attention to us children at all, even though we tried our best to win his friendship.

True, he never refused to take the apples, bread or other titbits we offered him, but each time he accepted them with a very scornful look, as if to show us he was doing us a terrible favour.

Two months passed. During this time Mishka became used to us and to his new surroundings. He was not as frightened of the dogs any more and often his walks would take him far from the house.

The white spots on his back and sides had

disappeared. He was beginning to shed. All baby deer and wild kids have these white spots which later disappear. There were now two little bumps on his forehead where his antlers would be one day.

Mother fed him very well, and Mishka became smooth and plump. He was growing very quickly, for he would drink more than a potful of milk at a time. Mother was beginning to worry.

"I don't know what to do. I have to feed him three times a day. If this keeps up, I won't have any milk for the children."

And so she began to add a little water to his milk. At first just a cupful and then more and more, until finally she would add only two or three cups of milk to a pail of water.

This didn't seem to bother Mishka at all, and he continued to drink with the greatest of pleasure. Then one day something seemed to have happened. When he was given his usual diluted milk he snorted and kicked over the pail, and from that day on he never touched another drop of milk, not even whole milk.

His childhood had ended. Now Mishka changed over to a different diet. He shared the cow's fodder and whenever the horses were given oats he tried to join them.

He was a bit afraid of the horses, for they could not stand to have him poking his nose into their trough and would often bite him.

To make up for this insult, Mishka thoroughly despised the cow. As soon as Mother set out the cow's fodder and went back into the house Mishka would pop out from nowhere, chase the cow away and start eating her food. Poor Buryonka would stand off to a side, watching him sadly.

"Oh, you scoundrel! What are you doing?" the grown-ups would shout if they came upon this highway robbery.

Mishka would jump at the unexpected shout, do several fancy leaps, sail over the fence and head for the hills.

Mishka had an excellent appetite and the treat he liked best were cigarette butts.

He would wander up and down under the forestry office windows collecting butts. He apparently liked to chew the tobacco in them and the cigarette paper, too.

Mishka was full of energy. He was always ready to run, jump and get into mischief. He would be walking around the yard quietly, then suddenly raise his head, flick his ears and with a *whoosh!* he would tear off around the house, down the road to the river and back up the hill, jumping over the rocks and fallen logs, kicking up his hind legs.

One day Mother hung out the washing to dry. Mishka was right behind her. He chose one of the largest sheets and calmly began chewing on a corner.

He stood there chewing for quite a while and then decided to visit the grove where we usually played.

He pulled the sheet off the line, tossed his head, throwing it over his shoulder, and set off in triumph past the house, dragging an end along the ground. Luckily, someone saw him and took the sheet away, but the damage was done. A huge part of the sheet was full of tiny holes and fell apart at a touch. This habit of chewing whatever he laid his eyes on was his most unpleasant one, and a rather expensive habit it was. Our curtains, table-cloths and kerchiefs all bore traces of Mishka's attention. He even chewed a huge round hole right in the middle of Yulia's best dress.

Oh, what there were that day!

Once, Father was looking for the key to the wardrobe.

It was not on the hook where it always hung. We all began looking for it and spent the whole day hunting in the house and in the yard, but it had vanished. We hated to break the lock, for it was a fine English lock which had a tiny key on a thin leather strap.

"Who could have taken the key? This is outrageous!" Father said angrily.

Finally, when we had lost all hope of ever finding it, Mother noticed a piece of rag dangling from the corner of Mishka's mouth.

She went over to him, got hold of the end and pulled. The rag turned out to be the leather key strap. Mishka had eaten half of it and had swallowed the key as well.

"He's a freak, that's what he is!" Father fumed.

We thought Mishka would get sick from such indigestible food, but he seemed to think the key was delicious and continued eating strange things.

Once, when we were tarring the horse's harness near the barn, Mishka managed to steal the saddle girth. Father noticed that he was chewing on a long white rope and pulled it out of his mouth. Mishka had a leather strap a yard long in his mouth with an iron ring in the middle of it.

After all that chewing, the stiff black strap had become as soft as a rag and as white as snow. The iron ring didn't seem to bother Mishka at all.

And so the summer passed and then the autumn and the winter. Mishka's second spring was fast approaching. He was now nine months old and was taller than a year-old calf. He was strong and fleet-footed. He liked to stroll in the groves and chew the young branches. That is why he probably held his head so high, for he was not used to bending down for grass.

His antlers had come through. At first, they were soft and hot and swollen. They were covered with fine down, like a ripe peach.

If Mishka stood with his back to the sun you could see the red blood in his antlers. While they were still soft he was meek and gentle. He would often come up to us and rub his head against us gently, asking us to stroke his antlers. They were hot and very tender. If we were not careful and patted them too hard, he would shudder and kick at us.

By then we had become fast friends, playing together for days on end. Whenever we set out for the forest or the mountains, Mishka would always tag along.

It was a strange procession: the four of us, the Kazakh children from the neighbouring village, five or six dogs and Mishka in the middle. He had never liked to be left alone, and now he was more attached to human beings than ever.

Once Yulia was teasing Mishka. Suddenly, she made believe she was frightened of him and ran away. Mishka ran after her. Yulia giggled as she dashed up the porch steps. Then she turned around and stuck out her tongue at him. Mishka raised his head and stuck his tongue out at her and he crinkled up his nose and hissed *ffff* besides! We were agape with wonder.

Good for Mishka!

After that we all began to tease him and then run to safety on the porch. Mishka immediately caught on to the game. He would trot away from the porch, stop and wait till someone came up to him with outstretched hands. Then he would launch an attack and chase them back up the porch. We shrieked with delight as we scrambled up the stairs in time to see Mishka raise his head, stick his tongue out of the side of his mouth and hiss. That was the best part of the game. It was also fun to have a deer chasing you.

We kept playing this game until Mishka's antlers became hard. Oh, how sorry we were then that we had taught him to chase us!

When his antlers became hard the fuzz that had covered them became stiff and matted and began to peel together with the skin. Mishka kept rubbing his antlers against tree trunks, trying to scrape off the "woollen" skin as quickly as possible. Finally, it was

54

all off. Mishka's first antlers were not very big and there were no side branchings at all.

The next year Mishka lost his first antlers. A second pair with two branchings on them grew in their place. Each year the number of branchings on a maral's antlers increases until the stag reaches its full maturity. This is how hunters guess a stag's age.

Mishka became terribly vain and marched around the house with his beautiful proud head held high.

One day, as he was parading around the yard, he stepped on Mailik's bowl and turned it over.

"Who are we to look underfoot? We're much too important for that!" Yulia said crossly.

Mailik was peeved to be deprived of his dinner. He curled back his lip and snarled at Mishka.

The result was most unexpected.

Instead of backing away in fright as he usually did, Mishka lowered his antlers, rushed at Mailik, pressed him against the barn wall, reared up and began battering the dog with his hoofs.

Mailik howled.

People came running at the sound of Yulia's screams and chased Mishka away.

From that day on the dogs were terrified of Mishka. They saved up all their grievances for spring, when Mishka lost his antlers, and then they had their revenge.

Once, when we were having water-melon for dessert, Natasha went outside to treat Mishka to the rind.

Suddenly we heard a shriek followed by screams.

We all ran out. There, in the middle of the yard, was Natasha, standing on all fours and screaming at the top of her voice. That good-for-nothing Mishka was pummelling her back with his sharp hoofs. Lying in the dust was the water-melon rind he had knocked out of her hands.

In an instant Mailik forgot his fear of Mishka. He sank his teeth into the deer's hind leg. By then everyone came running to Natasha's rescue.

When Mishka saw Sonya hurrying to her sister's aid, he hopped aside, bowed, jumped over the fence and headed for the hills.

We finally calmed Natasha down and asked her what had happened. We realised from what she told us that it had all been a terrible mistake and that Mishka had mistaken her intentions.

In our old game we had always teased Mishka by waggling our fingers under his nose. And now, when Natasha had come up to him offering the water-melon rind, Mishka had thought she was poking her fingers at him and had become terribly offended.

"Shame on you! First you tease the animal and then you wonder why it fights back," Father said. "Wait till his antlers get harder, he'll show you a thing or two!"

Mishka did not return until late that night. Father put him in the stable and punished him by keeping him there for several days. In the mornings Mishka would sigh sadly as he stuck his head out of the stable window. He would have loved to run and jump, and perhaps even to have had a nice fight. But here he was, locked up and punished.

Two days later he was angry and impatient as he paced back and forth inside the stable.

"Sonya," I said, "Mishka must be hungry. Let's give him something to eat."

"He's not hungry at all. I just gave him some oats."

But I felt Mishka was not being treated properly.

"I'll go up to the hayloft and throw him down some hay," I finally decided.

So up I went. I gathered an armful of hay and began looking for a wide crack in the log floor where I could push the hay down into the stable.

I walked about the hayloft searching for a crack until suddenly I fell through a big hole in the floor and landed next to Mishka, hay and all!

Now Mishka would have his revenge! He rose up on his hind legs and began battering my head until he nearly cracked my skull. Luckily, Sonya came running up with a whip and hit him hard to make him stop.

I wasn't friends with Mishka any more for a long time afterwards. Mishka was soon let out of the stable, but instead of feeling sorry for what he had done he became worse than ever.

There was a tiny cottage on Shaggy Mountain where an old man lived all by himself. He had a small bee garden near his cottage and he had planted a large field of wild flowers in the meadow nearby to keep the bees from flying too far away in their search for nectar.

During his wanderings Mishka had discovered the cottage and now decided to pay the old man a visit.

One day, when the old man was sitting on a bench and quietly weaving baskets, he heard the sound of breaking glass. First Mishka's antlers and then his head came through the window.

What could that be?! The old man began mumbling "Holy! Holy! Holy!" hastily, but Mishka only twitched his ears. He had no intention of vanishing.

The old man peeped out of the door. He was awed by Mishka's beauty.

"I would really be like a holy man if I could only tame this scoundrel," he said to himself, thinking of his broken window. "He's just as beautiful as the animals in my religious pictures."

He found a piece of bread and called to Mishka: "Here, boy! Here, boy!"

Mishka disentangled his head from the window, came up to the old man, sniffed at the bread and ate it with pleasure.

Then the old man put a handful of salt on the bench for him.

Ah! Mishka knew all about salt! He loved it and began licking it up with such pleasure that he left a whole puddle of saliva on the bench.

When he had finished the salt the bench looked freshly scrubbed.

This is how they became acquainted.

The old man was very pleased and proud of himself. Certainly, he must be a very good, kind man, he thought, if even wild beasts sensed his goodness and came up to him as tame as lambs and did not want to leave.

Mishka surveyed the house and the yard and then lay down on the low earthen roof of the cellar, where he fell asleep. He always chose the most uncomfortable spots to sleep in.

The happy old man went back to weaving his baskets.

In the daytime Mishka would go away to the forest, but he would come back to spend the night at his new friend's house. This continued for about ten days. Sometimes Mishka would come home for a few hours and then disappear again.

At home we had all become accustomed to Mishka's constant wanderings and were not the least bit worried.

The old bee-keeper was still good to Mishka, though, to tell the truth, he would not have been too disappointed if the stag he thought he had tamed had taken himself off for good.

The reason for this change of heart was simple enough: Mishka had already chewed up the cloth the old man used on his table, as well as a piece of his coat and his leather belt; he had trampled the flowers and, finally, he had sailed over the fence into the enclosure where the beehives were. There he began prancing about until he had toppled over every single one of them. The old man had patiently tried to overlook all this, but he was getting very angry.

Once, he set out to gather firewood for the winter. Since his cottage was right in the middle of the forest, the old man never locked his door when he went away. This suited Mishka fine.

The moment the old man disappeared behind the trees, Mishka entered the cottage to have a look around. The walls were covered with brightly coloured pictures of Biblical scenes.

Mishka gazed intently at "St. George and the Dragon". Here was a picture after his own heart. He got a corner of it between his lips, pulled at it and chewed off the dragon and St. George's legs. His gaze then wandered to "The Flood" where he greedily consumed both saints and sinners. He merely tore "Adam and Eve Driven from Eden" off the wall and tossed them to the floor. He was just about to go on to the next picture when he heard the old man singing in the distance.

Mishka sensed that here, as at home, no one would really be overjoyed at his chewing. His only thought was to escape as quickly as possible, but the ceiling was so low and the cottage so small that he couldn't properly turn around in it, for by now he was nearly as big as a horse and his antlers were fairly large. The only way he could get out was to back out through the door. But by then the old man was at the door. He saw the shreds of his pictures and realised what had happened.

"Oh, you shaggy devil! Oh, you miserable wretch!" the angry old man shouted. He picked up a heavy stick and hit the heathen deer on the back. Mishka was offended and ran away.

Several days later he was back, wandering about the cottage again. The old man did not see him, as he was busy in the bee garden. When Mishka saw him bend over a beehive, he stole up from behind, reared up and beat the old man with his hoofs. No question about it; it was enough to try the patience of a saint!

The old man cursed the "miserable wretch" and chased Mishka away.

Summer had ended. The leaves had fallen from the trees, hoar-frost covered the ground in the mornings. It would soon be winter.

With the coming of cold weather life in the mountain village seemed to stop. The people stayed indoors most of the time. Sometimes we would not see a soul for days on end.

Then the first snow fell.

Mishka greeted it excitedly. He did an intricate dance in the snow, then pranced about, pulling down the lower branches of the trees, shaking clouds of snow onto his back, and trampling it; finally, feeling all hot and flustered, he began gulping down great mouthfuls of it.

It was only now that we realised what a heavy coat of fur he had grown for the winter. The fur was especially long and thick on his neck, as if he had put on a beautiful warm collar. There was a fringe on his chest and along the bottom of his stomach but his legs remained as thin and sleek and furless as in summer.

This is what distinguishes a maral from a reindeer. A reindeer's legs are shorter and thicker, with a fringe of fur around the hoof. His shaggy legs are like fur boots, while the maral seems to be walking on high heels in all seasons.

Mishka managed to keep out of trouble all winter long. True, he would often leave the yard to go wandering in the woods and mountains or would follow the road down to the deserted summer cottages, but he was always home by evening. He slept on a mat on the roof of the smithy, shielded by an overhanging ledge of the hill.

Sometimes Mishka would head towards the nearest village, but he always came racing back with a pack of dogs yelping at his heels.

Taking several turns round the house, Mishka would stop at the porch, lower his antlers and plunge into battle. Then the pack would fall away yelping, while Mishka kicked or butted the more persistent and courageous dogs.

When the first breath of spring began to melt the snow, Mishka became very sad and spent most of his time in the forest.

He began to shed in February. His beautiful grey-brown fur became matted and fell off in clumps. He lost his antlers and his face took on a lost and helpless look.

The first streams began to gurgle, snowdrops and violets bloomed in sunny places. Then the fields and trees turned green and we all came out of the house. Our singing and shouting could be heard through the mountains.

This was a time for happy journeys to begin again.

Mishka was nervous, he kept losing weight and was very gloomy.

As spring turned into summer the little bumps on his head began to swell again. Poor Mishka suffered terribly from the flies and horseflies that came to suck the blood from his new antlers. He would crawl into a dark corner of the barn and spend his days there, feeling miserable, and would only come out in the evening to nibble leaves and tender shoots in a nearby grove.

Mother felt terribly sorry for Mishka. She tried rubbing some ointment on his tender young antlers to keep the flies away, but it only irritated them.

She often treated him to tasty snacks to make him feel better. Mishka was grateful and loved her best of all. He obeyed her every command and followed her around like a dog.

He loved to lie at her feet when she sat sewing or knitting on the porch. Often he would rest his sad face on her shoulder and stand there with his eyes closed, as his mistress patted him gently. Mother was always the first to defend him whenever he got into mischief.

Now she began to worry for fear that one of the hunters who came to the mountains might shoot him, thinking Mishka was a wild stag. So she made him a leather collar and tied two large red and blue bows to it.

But even though you could see the bright bows from afar, they did not save Mishka from disaster.

This is how it happened.

A naturalist who, they said, had come from the

capital set up a tent and broke camp two kilometres up the canyon.

He spent his days wandering about the mountains, taking pictures, collecting pebbles and grasses on the way.

In the evening he would return to his tent to cook his supper and pore over his finds, later packing them away in little boxes.

Mishka discovered the tent when the man was out. At first, he tried to knock it over. Then he came upon some scraps of paper and cigarette butts, ate them and decided that the tent was not such a bad thing after all and that he would drop by again.

When Mishka crawled out of his dark barn the next evening he set off for the tent. The flaps were thrown back and he stuck his curious nose inside.

To his great misfortune the naturalist was in.

Goodness! The brave hunter was so frightened he did not even notice the bright red and blue bows on Mishka's collar and quite forgot that a wild deer would never come so close to a human being. He grabbed up his gun frantically and shot Mishka point-blank.

Mishka fell.

A forester passing by heard the shot and came to the rescue.

He saw Mishka in convulsions on the ground and the naturalist standing over him with a puzzled expression as he examined the bows on his collar. The forest guard headed straight for our house.

"Hurry! There's been an accident! Mishka's been killed!" he shouted as he came running into the yard. In his haste Father tore the hitching rope, grabbed his gun and set off for the tent in a rage. Mother was afraid he might do something rash and ran after him.

She came to the tent just as Father was telling the naturalist what he thought of him. The man, crimson with embarrassment, was mumbling his apologies.

"I wonder where you city fellows keep your brains! Don't you know a wild deer will never stick his head into a tent! Some naturalist you are!"

Luckily, the naturalist was such a wonderful marksman that even though he had shot Mishka point-blank between the eyes he had missed and had hit his antler instead, chipping off a piece of one of the branches which now hung by a shred of skin.

Father rolled up his sleeves and got set to operate.

The naturalist brought out his first-aid kit, then ran for a pail of water and tried to be as helpful as possible to make up for what he had done.

They removed the broken piece as well as a part of the antler. Mishka shrieked horribly. The blood gushed forth with such force that it spattered a tree growing four feet away.

Finally, it was all over. Father poured some disinfectant on the wound. Mishka dropped his head in utter exhaustion and seemed to have lost consciousness.

He lay there moaning all night long under a piece of canvas.

The next day he got up and hobbled home with Father supporting him.

That year his antlers looked rather strange: one was normal, while half of the other was missing.

We thought that from then on his antlers would always be uneven. But we were wrong.

Next spring Mishka shed his unsightly antlers and by July he had grown a beautiful, branching new pair.

Mishka was now going on five.

He really outdid himself that summer. As soon as the fruit ripened in the orchards that surrounded the summer cottages, Mishka began spending his days there.

He would go far down the road towards town, choose a spot to his liking, sail over the fence, grab a branch between his teeth and shake it. The apples would come raining down. Mishka would then eat two or three and go on to the next tree. He did not eat as much as he spoiled.

When the owners would see a carpet of crushed half-ripened fruit beneath their trees in the morning they would become furious.

They soon discovered that the stag belonged to us and began coming to our house to complain.

"But what can I do?" Father would say helplessly. "Chase him away yourselves!"

He tried to lock Mishka up to punish him, but Mishka was a freedom-loving animal and being locked up only made him mean.

We could always expect new developments from the "battle-field", as Father called the town orchards.

Indeed, reports of Mishka's sorties were not long in coming: yesterday he had fought with the children of some people who had just moved in, today he had pulled someone's dress off the line and had chewed it to shreds, and the day before yesterday, while prancing on the roof of someone's earthen cellar, he had fallen through and had knocked over all the jugs of milk cooling there.

"What are we to do? He's a real bandit!" Mother and Father grieved.

Finally, after receiving a severe beating from someone, Mishka calmed down and began spending more of his time closer to home.

We breathed a sigh of relief, but our peace was short-lived.

Once, Mishka came home with a huge yoke and harness on his antlers. He had probably come upon them near a wagon and had butted the yoke. Then his antlers had got stuck in it and when he saw that he could not pull them out, he became frightened and galloped home.

We all burst out laughing as he came galloping up to the house with this strange contraption on his head. We took off the yoke and Father hung out a notice, but since the owner never turned up, the yoke became part of our household belongings and was always referred to as "Mishka's yoke".

The next event took place several weeks later. This time Mishka went visiting his old friend the bee-keeper and came back with the man's sheepskin coat on his antlers. We were working in the garden when we suddenly saw Mishka marching down the road proudly with a heavy fur coat draped over his head. Trotting along beside him, shouting and cursing angrily, was the old man.

We cornered Mishka in the yard, took away the coat and gave it back to the old man. He looked at Mishka with loathing, and told him he hoped he would drop dead, the sooner the better. Mishka, however, had no such intentions.

Since we had grown up together we were used to Mishka and not at all afraid of him. When he shed his antlers in the spring and became helpless we would feel sorry for him, spoil him, and feel that we were his defenders. That is why, as soon as Mishka had grown his new pair of antlers and would try to show us how strong he was, instead of running away we would say firmly:

"Stop that, silly! Don't be a bully!"

But strangers were afraid of him and would turn and run in terror. Mishka would always catch up with them and give them a good thrashing.

One day a large group of well-dressed young ladies and gentlemen came for a picnic in the mountains. Soon they were wandering about the forest. One couple was sitting and chatting gaily under a large pine tree when suddenly the young lady turned and saw Mishka walking towards them.

"Help! Help! He'll kill us! Look, he's getting closer! Help! What shall we do?" she cried.

And with a frantic scream the young lady ran to a nearby tree, grabbed hold of a branch and hung there like a large plum.

The gentleman decided to defend his young lady.

He took off his cap and waved it at Mishka, thinking that would scare him away.

Mishka raised his head, stuck out his tongue and hissed.

The brave young man then threw a pine cone at him. But when Mishka took another step towards him he suddenly turned heel and ran down the mountain as fast as he could. Mishka meanwhile decided to have another look at the young lady.

The unfortunate damsel, seeing how swiftly her defender was disappearing in the distance, let go of the branch in terror and fell right at Mishka's feet.

He did one of his most intricate dances around her and was just about to conclude it by giving her a good thrashing when Sonya came running to her rescue and chased him away.

There was never a dull day all summer long. In between mischief-making, Mishka would amuse himself by fighting with the dogs, racing about in the mountains or swimming in the river. His idea of swimming was to stand in the middle of the river and churn up the water by beating the surface with his front legs.

One of the games we liked was to hide on the porch with a small pail of water and wait till Mishka passed by. Then we would jump out and douse him.

What a dance he would do then!

He was six years old when he left the house one morning and was gone for two whole months. Mother was despondent. She was sure someone had shot him.

She should not have worried. One day Father was returning from his rounds and saw a group of cows pressing close together in a circle. They seemed hypnotised and mooed in wonder from time to time. Mishka was in the middle of the circle, doing a dance for them. He seemed very pleased to have impressed so many cows at once and was really outdoing himself. He spun about, lowered his antlers, bent his knees, reared up on his hind legs and pranced this way and that, bowing to all sides.

"Oh, you scoundrel!" Father said, laughing. He was glad to see that Mishka was not only hale and hearty, but in good spirits as well.

At the sound of Father's voice Mishka started, leaped over the cows and ran home. The next few days he was more gentle and sweet than he had ever been before, and Mother was too pleased for words. Father was told that a small herd of marals had been spotted in the vicinity. He warned us that Mishka would probably leave us for good now.

Mother would not believe him. She said he would just visit them and then he would come back again, but Mishka did go. He went beyond the mountain pass with them and never came back. He was now at an age when a stag is ready to fight the whole world to win his mate. Mishka was a great and mighty stag and

we consoled ourselves by thinking that he would
certainly vanquish all his rivals. He would be the
leader of the herd.

Farewell, Mishka! Good luck!

ISHKA AND MILKA

My sister and I had just come home from school. The house was empty, as everyone was working in the garden. We ran right out again, taking our honour certificates with us.

"Good for you!" Mother said. "Congratulations! How nice to have received your first prizes! Father and I should really give you something nice for such good work. What do you say, Father?"

Sonya nudged me, saying:

"Tell them about...."

I coughed from excitement.

"We don't want any presents!" I blurted.

"Why not?"

"It's not that we really don't want any presents, but could you give us a ruble each instead? We're going to keep getting prizes from now on. We're saving up to buy a donkey."

"When did you start saving? How much have you saved already?"

"We started last winter and have a ruble fifty-five," Natasha said proudly. Although she was only five, we had chosen her to be our treasurer, for she was the most thrifty of us all.

"Exactly a ruble fifty-five. Want me to show you?"

"Are you in on it, too? You don't go to school, and you don't get any lunch money."

"I put the fifteen kopecks I found near the gate in the kitty."

Father stuck his spade into a vegetable bed and looked through his pockets.

"I see you've got a going concern and I'd like to have a share in it. Will you take me on as a partner? Here's my five rubles. It'll be my share. Now get your savings and off you go to the market!"

"What? Right now? Today?"

Half an hour later we were tramping barefoot down the hot, dusty road, heading for the livestock market. Sonya led the procession. She was carrying the money, trying hard not to drop or lose any of it. I walked beside her, my eyes never leaving her hand. Drawing up the rear were our younger sisters, Yulia and Natasha, chatting gaily and laughing as they hurried along.

At times we were suddenly gripped by a terrible

fear. We would stop in the middle of the road, Sonya would unclench her hot fist and we would see that the damp, crumpled paper was really five rubles, that we still had it and that we would have a real live donkey of our own this very day.

The market-place was at the other end of town. We crossed cool, shady streets and scorching squares. The dust was so hot it hurt our feet. We would race across the hot squares and then sit down by the side of irrigation ditches to cool our burning feet in the water.

The livestock market was situated in the middle of just such a square. We could hear the many-voiced roars of the animals from afar, the sound of whips cracking and the shouts of the drivers. The whole square seemed alive from the masses of cows, horses and sheep being led back and forth.

We were pressed tight in the commotion and did not know what to do.

"Look! There's Petya! Pe-e-tya-a!" we shouted.

"What are you yelling for? And what are you doing here anyway?" our neighbour's son asked, coming up to us. He pulled his cap down over his eyes, trying to look more important.

But he knew exactly why we were there, for he had followed us all the way from home and was only pretending he knew nothing.

"So you want to buy a donkey? Well, all I can say is you need somebody who knows the business, otherwise they'll cheat you sure as anything."

"What about you, Petya? You know all about donkeys, don't you?"

"Well, I might help you at that. But what was the use of coming down here and not telling me? Why, they'd have made monkeys of you in no time. They'd have sold a sick donkey and you'd never even know it."

We listened to him in horror, imagining what might have happened. We were as meek as lambs after that.

"Well, Petya, we're certainly lucky we found you. You always seem to turn up at the right time."

We walked up and down the market stalls.

"Are you selling this donkey?"

"Yes."

"How much?"

"Ten rubles."

"I'll give you three."

"Idiot!"

Petya was so wonderful at bargaining that men were soon cursing him from all sides.

"Petya, look! See that big black donkey over there? That's the kind we want."

"How much do you want for him?"

"Seven rubles."

"Would you sell him for six and a ha...."

"If you're going to stick your nose in I'm leaving!" Petya screamed at Sonya. "Then you can do whatever you want!"

Sonya said no more. He turned to the man again.

"Top price for a donkey like this is four rubles."

"All right, you can have him."

Sonya unclenched her fist.

"Wait! Wait, Sonya! You'll have plenty of time to get rid of your money. We have to try him out first. Maybe he's no good."

"You're right. Go on, Petya, get on him and see how good he is."

We sat down to watch. Petya got on the donkey and tried to make him gallop, but the donkey turned out to be lame.

And so we began our search again. Suddenly, I spotted a small grey donkey. He was standing sadly to one side burdened with two huge bundles of firewood that reached to the ground and all but hid him from view. There was that huge pile of firewood and peeping out from under it was a small grey head with large intelligent eyes and soft, velvety ears.

"What a darling he is!" Yulia said, pointing to him.

"He's so shy. He's just standing there with his tail hanging down!" Natasha said happily.

"I don't think anyone would sell a donkey like that."

"Maybe they will. Let's ask."

We did ask and discovered that the donkey really was for sale.

"How much?"

"Eight rubles."

Five voices joined in begging the man to lower his price. Oh, how we pleaded with him! Petya offered him his hand to clinch the deal a dozen times, Natasha gazed into his eyes gently, while Sonya kept repeating:

"Six and a half, all right? All right?"

Finally, the heavy bundles of wood were lifted off the donkey's back and we were solemnly presented with an end of the rope that was tied around his neck.

The road home seemed twice as short. We all talked at once and kept laughing for no reason at all.

"Here we are! We're back!" Sonya shouted as she ran on ahead to open the gate. Petya was the first to enter. Yulia and I were both holding the end of the rope, while Natasha rode the donkey.

Everyone was pleased with the purchase, but when all was said and done we discovered we had bought a female donkey instead of male.

"That's even better. Just think how many baby donkeys we'll have!"

We named her Ishka. She was still very young and small, not more than a year old, at best, and about as big as a calf. Kazakhstan donkeys are usually never more than a metre high.

Ishka stood under the porch, happily munching on the hard cookies Natasha had been hoarding since Christmas, while we all stood around, admiring and patting her.

Ishka was as grey as a mouse, with a fluffy little brush at the tip of her tail. There was a black stripe running from the very tip to her ears. It crossed another black stripe at her shoulders.

Her short, stiff, curly mane and long twitching ears were also black, while her soft, satiny belly, nose and legs were white.

We picked the burs out of her tail and mane and combed and brushed her.

Ishka looked pretty now and seemed sweeter than ever. There was a tuft of hair on her forehead that came down to her eyes and made her look as if she were peeping out from under her brows.

We took her into the orchard, found a place where the grass grew thickest and left her there to graze.

Ishka nibbled some grass, glanced at us and set off for the back yard determinedly with her head bobbing up and down in time to her steps. The garbage pit was in the back yard with nettles and thistles growing everywhere. We were puzzled as we followed Ishka. What could she have seen of interest there? Ishka began by tearing off a huge prickly leaf and chewing it.

"Oh, take it away from her! Hurry!" Natasha shouted. "Oh, my poor Ishka! Your stomach will be all full of prickles."

We tried to take the leaf away but Ishka got angry. She pressed her ears close to her skull and shook her head at us.

"Wait!" Sonya cried and ran to find Father and ask him what was wrong. Did Ishka want to poison herself with the thistles?

Sonya was soon back. She pushed us aside and said:

"Let the animal do as it wishes. It will never eat anything that will harm it. Donkeys live in tropical countries where the sun burns out the grass, but thistles grow abundantly there. They're not harmful at all, because they're juicy and tasty. And don't worry about the prickles, they won't stick Ishka."

Sonya explained it all so cleverly and she looked so important you would think she had known about it all along. There was a crowd of children in the back yard, and they all listened to her with open mouths. Finally, I could stand it no longer and said:

"You're a show-off, Sonya! Why, you just found it out yourself! And who cares about tropical countries? This isn't a tropical country!"

I was so hot and bothered that my neck felt damp. A swarm of flies and bees was buzzing over the garbage pit. Ishka raised clouds of dust as she rolled around in a pile of ashes.

Sonya did not bat an eye at my grumbling and continued discussing donkeys in a very learned manner.

Towards evening we finished building a little pen. We had a basket for a trough and spread some straw on the ground. Then we led Ishka into the pen. She did

not like her new quarters at all. During the night,
when everyone was asleep, she squeezed under one
of the boards with a grunt and was soon out in the
yard. The horses were eating their clover and snorting
loudly near the barn; the cow was standing in the
middle of the yard; the sleeping dogs looked like furry
balls.

Ishka walked among them, nudging them with her
nose. The dogs growled in their sleep, but she kept at
them until she had finally got them all up and barking
crossly at her. She put back her ears, bared her teeth
and bobbed her head, as if to say: "You don't know
me yet! But you had better watch your step when I'm
around!"

Then Ishka noticed the cow. She walked up to it
from behind and bit its leg. The cow kicked out,

82

turned its head and lowered its horns. Then Ishka showed herself to be a truly terrible beast: she stiffened, bared her teeth and began kicking and biting the poor old cow until it finally set off at a gallop with Ishka hot on its heels.

After this, all Ishka had to do was twist her tail and the cow would be off like a rocket.

This was just what Ishka had been hoping for.

After all, she really had no means of protection: neither fangs, nor claws, nor horns, and no one would ever be frightened at the sight of her little hoofs. The animals might easily have got the better of her, if she had not been so bold and persistent. But Ishka was very independent and all the animals respected her. Some were even afraid of her, because clever Ishka acted so fiercely and attacked her enemies so boldly that they fell back in spite of themselves.

We did not ride Ishka the first week, because we wanted her to get used to us. We patted her and fed her bread and sugar and soon Ishka knew each and every one of us. It was quite obvious that she liked Yulia and Natasha best. They spent all their days fussing about her, trimming her tail, combing her mane and polishing her hoofs.

Once, Sonya and I were bathing the horse. We tied it to a hitching post and poured water from the irrigation ditch on it. The horse liked its bath. True, it would roll a wary eye whenever we raised the pail over its back, but it would snort happily and do a little

6*

jig, treading imaginary water as the little streams trickled down its sides.

Just as we were through bathing the horse, we saw Yulia and Natasha pulling Ishka along. They tied her to the post and began bathing her, too.

But Ishka would have none of it. She jerked and yanked at the rope, and each time the water came down on her back she kicked out in the funniest way.

Now, when she was soaking wet, she looked like a plucked chicken: her neck was thin, her head was big and fuzzy, her legs were as skinny as matchsticks and her belly was as big and round as a water-melon.

As soon as Yulia would raise the basin, Ishka would begin to pull and jerk, neatly avoiding the water.

"Natasha, bring her over here and hold her. I'm going to douse her from the ditch," Yulia said.

She stepped over the ditch and stood above it, with one foot on either side. Then she scooped up a basinful of water. Natasha untied Ishka and led her over to the ditch. She had the rope in one hand and a bun in the other.

Yulia threw the water on Ishka and bent down to fill the basin again.

By then Ishka was in a rage and flew at Yulia. Yulia cried out, dropped the basin into the ditch, slipped and fell right into the basin!

Yulia was now floating downstream in the basin. We laughed so loudly that the horse bolted, Natasha choked on a mouthful of bun, Ishka grabbed what was left of it and made a dash for the barn.

We were still laughing as we ran to the rescue. On the way we pounded Natasha on the back to bring up the piece she had choked on, while the neighbours' boys fished Yulia and the basin out farther downstream. She was drenched to the skin and had hurt her knee, but the moment her feet touched the ground she said:

"Where's Ishka? Oh, you muddleheads!"

Meanwhile, Ishka was back rolling around to her heart's delight in her favourite cinders. After a while she got up and shook herself.

"I guess living in tropical countries doesn't teach donkeys to bathe," Sonya said thoughtfully.

We made a bridle and saddle for Ishka from straps and a piece of heavy felt. When everything was ready we put on the harness and saddle and began riding her.

She trotted very nicely in what is known as "dog-pacing" style, and she also galloped swiftly and lightly. But whenever she was in a bad mood, or if she happened to dislike the person who was riding her, she'd go into an impossible bone-shattering trot that made your teeth rattle. We called this her "rumble-tumble" trot.

Soon after we had begun riding her we hung up the harness and saddle in the barn and never took them down again, since we guided Ishka with a little twig or our hands. If we tapped her on the right side of her neck she would turn to the left, and if we tapped her on the left side, she would turn to the right. When we wanted her to stop we would gently tug a tuft of hair between her ears and she would stop. If we tugged a tuft of hair on her side that meant full steam ahead. Then Ishka would start right off at a gallop.

Yulia and Natasha rode Ishka very well and liked to ride her. Sonya and I were not as lucky, for Ishka was never in a hurry to obey our commands. She kicked and always rode us "rumble-tumble" so that we felt our insides were upside down.

Once I was sent to look for our strayed baby turkeys.

"You don't mount her correctly," Yulia said. "You have to sit further back from the neck. Over here." And she smacked Ishka on the rump to show me.

I followed her instructions and found myself sitting practically on top of Ishka's tail. I had a very short guide stick and could not reach Ishka's neck, so she set out at her own pace, which happened to be a full gallop.

As we were rattling along I inched forward. Suddenly, Ishka stopped dead and lowered her head to the ground. And off I flew.

She then turned around and galloped down the middle of the road towards home, tossing her head back proudly, turning it now to the left, now to the right as she brayed triumphantly: "*Hee-haw! Hee-haw! Hee-haw!*" Yes, she thought she had really done a very fine thing!

Sonya never liked to ride Ishka either.

"Where's the animal's saddle?" she would say doubtfully as she stared at Ishka's perfectly straight back. "At least when you ride a horse you know you have to sit on the saddle. But here you might as well be sitting on her tail."

Yulia and Natasha were never bothered by such technical problems. They would trot around on Ishka all day long, either one at a time or both together, and sometimes they would take on one of the neighbour's children as a third passenger.

Ishka was so used to them that she followed them around like a dog. It was very convenient to have your own means of transportation so close at hand.

Once, when we were sweeping the yard, I went over to speak to Sonya, leaving my broom near the gate, about thirty feet away.

Natasha was standing next to me. In all seriousness she mounted Ishka, rode across the yard and brought back my broom.

Mother saw this and laughed heartily. "Why, my dears, at this rate you'll soon forget how to walk!" she said.

Ishka brought many changes into our life.

Before she came, for instance, if Mother wanted one of us to go to a shop or the market in town there would never be a soul in sight. She would have to call us again and again, and finally she would plead:

"Yulia dear, don't you love your Mamma?"

"I don't know," her loving daughter would reply. "Please don't send me to the market. I'll go to the shop for you, if you give me a candy."

Oh, everything was quite different now.

"Mamma, are you sure you don't need anything at the market?"

"Mamma, can we go shopping for you?" the girls would say several times a day.

If Yulia had to go to town for sugar and thread, Natasha would see her off to the gate and whisper:

"Now don't forget!"

Then little grey Ishka would go trotting across town and Yulia's little red hat would go bobbing up and down above her.

But when she came back, Mother would discover that she had forgotten to buy the thread. For some strange reason Natasha was always close by with her hat on her head, ready to leave.

And once again a little grey donkey would go

trotting down the streets with another little red hat bobbing up and down above it.

Ishka made our games much more interesting. Now, for instance, if we were playing a game about India, we would adorn Ishka with feathers, bits of bright rags and shiny paper. Then we'd put a little carpet on her back with a pillow on top of it and Natasha would sit on the pillow.

This made Ishka an elephant and Natasha a maharajah.

If a prisoner had to make a quick getaway it could now be done in true-to-life fashion on donkey-back.

Before, our distant journeys had been awful, for we had had to make believe that the sticks we rode were horses. Now, everything was different: we would load a tent, provisions and a pot in which to cook potatoes on Ishka.

The leader of the group would blaze the way, the pack horses would follow (Ishka was the pack horses), with the other adventurers bringing up the rear.

We set out for the mountains to gather apples and mushrooms and went on many other excursions besides.

We also had races. Sonya or I would mount the old pacer Gnedoi and challenge Ishka to a race of about two blocks. We lived on the outskirts of town and a meadow began beyond our orchard. That was where we had our races.

Many were the times when Ishka came flying to the finish first. But even then it was her cunning that got her first place.

We would line them up side by side.

"One! Two! Three!"

The pacer would charge straight ahead, while Ishka, with her tail tucked between her legs and the brush on the tip of it twirling, did her best to get right under Gnedoi's neck. If she succeeded, victory was hers, for she would never let him pass her. The old pacer would have to slow down, then he would try to nip the annoying creature that was kicking up its heels in front of him.

We once discovered the front axle of a little cart amidst the junk in back of the barn. As the two front wheels and shafts were perfectly sound, we managed to get together all the other necessary parts. With the help of our elders we put together a two-wheeled cart.

Ishka was most surprised when she was hitched to it. She kept turning back to see what that thing in back of her was, but she did not kick or protest. However, she hated the harness and would suddenly become mean and stubborn. If we pulled the right rein she would shake her head and turn left. So we had to forget about the reins and use a twig to guide her as before.

One day we were about to go to the market and decided to ride in the cart. We hitched Ishka to it, Yulia got on her back to guide her, while Natasha and

I climbed in. The road was downhill and Ishka trotted along easily. The wheels turned faster and faster, and the cloud of dust that rose behind us was exactly like the dust made by a real wagon.

When we got to the market-place we began riding up and down between the rows, picking out water-melons and cantaloupes for dinner. We spotted a huge water-melon and began bargaining with the man who was selling it. We were so busy haggling that we completely forgot about Ishka. Suddenly, I looked up to see that she was half-way through a basket of grapes. I nudged Yulia. She gasped and smacked Ishka with her twig.

Ishka bolted and knocked Natasha over. She had been holding the water-melon which fell and cracked.

Other traders came running up, shouting:

"Pay for the melon! Pay for the grapes!"

They said we owed them nearly all the money we had for all our purchases.

"We didn't do it on purpose."

"Yes, you did. Pay up, or you'll be sorry!"

What could we do? We had to pay them.

We were sad and silent on the way home, for we felt that we would never be sent to the market again. As if that were not enough, Ishka was up to her old tricks. She was pretending that she could hardly drag the cart. She strained at the harness, bent her head to the ground and twisted her ears until they nearly touched on the top of her head. All this meant the load was too heavy. I got off the cart and walked beside her, but Ishka kept twitching her ears.

Then we decided to fool her. Ishka didn't notice the other girls slip off the cart, but she kept behaving as if the load was still too great. We were really annoyed.

"Stop lying! Don't tell us you can't pull an empty cart. We'll really be in trouble when we get home and it's all your fault. Come on, girls, let's get back in."

When we all got in, Ishka stopped.

"What's the matter?"

"Maybe something's wrong?"

We walked around the cart and stood next to her. Then we saw that Ishka was staring at something shiny near her hoof. It was a five-ruble gold piece!

"Hurrah for Ishka!" we shouted.

We turned back to the market, bought everything on our list, treated Ishka to a snack and set out for home once again. Ishka trotted along smartly and we sang songs all the way.

In the winter we harnessed Ishka to a sledge. Then it was spring and we could no longer ride in the sledge or in the cart, or on Ishka, for the mud reached up to her knees.

Ishka had nothing to do for the next two months, but she was never bored. There were many donkeys at the brick factory nearby, and Ishka became acquainted with them. She would go off to visit them every day.

As soon as the ground dried we began roaming the countryside again. Ishka always went with us. But one day Father said:

"Don't get Ishka too tired, because she's going to have a little donkey soon."

"What do you mean?"

"Just what I said. She's going to have a baby donkey."

Natasha looked at Yulia.

"Since you wouldn't let me ride Ishka, she's going to give me a donkey of my own. It'll be even better than Ishka. Don't you think she knew I was jealous?"

We all agreed that Ishka certainly knew about that.

"Just wait and see," Natasha continued, "my donkey will be a real beauty! I won't let anyone ride him, so you might as well not ask."

From that day on she began taking very good care of Ishka. She fed her and kept watch to see that no one bothered her or frightened her. If someone had to go somewhere on Ishka, she would start arguing:

"Why do you have to ride Ishka? What's the matter? Can't you walk? See, she's closing her eyes. Maybe she's sick."

At first, we awaited the baby donkey from day to day. As soon as Natasha woke up in the morning she would run to Ishka, and as soon as she came back we would all say: "Well?"

"No. I guess she'll have her baby tomorrow."

Summer slipped into autumn, then it snowed. Sonya and I had been going to school for quite a while, but still there was no baby donkey.

Then Natasha began to have her doubts.

"I guess she's forgotten. Or maybe she's unhappy about something. Father promised us a baby donkey nearly a year ago, but she can't seem to get around to it."

Natasha tried to talk it over with Ishka, but it was no use. Finally, she stopped going to see her.

Early that spring Ishka's stomach got very big. She stopped teasing the cow and the dogs, walked about carefully and spent most of the day sunning herself. She'd go off to the garden, find a dry spot and stand there sunning herself.

One day Father said: "You have to be very careful with Ishka now. Her time will come soon."

94

The words were no sooner out of his mouth than Yulia burst into the room shouting: "Hurry! In the garden!"

We all tumbled out of the house. There, in a little hollow where the cucumbers grew in the summer, was a lovely little black donkey. Ishka was frantically trying to raise it up by prodding it with her nose. Father wanted to help her, but she screeched with rage and rushed at him. We suddenly noticed that the little donkey was lying very still.

Father thought this was very strange. He picked up a stick, chased Ishka off and bent over the foal. The little donkey was dead. Father picked him up and carried him off.

The donkey had been born hale and hearty, but he was Ishka's first-born, and she had accidentally killed him. Perhaps she had been frightened, or perhaps she had been careless. We later discovered that this happens to many animals when they have their first babies.

We followed Father to the field in silence. Ishka wanted to come with us but we wouldn't let her.

We buried the foal and went back home. Suddenly, we realised that Natasha was gone. She had not gone to the field with us, for when we had discovered that Ishka had killed her own baby, Natasha had disappeared.

We began looking for her. I went into the dark stable and found Natasha sitting in a corner under the trough, crying, while Ishka stood beside her, licking the tears from her face.

"Go away!" Natasha sobbed, pushing her away. "Stupid, crazy animal! You killed my little baby donkey!" And she sobbed as if her heart would break.

Another year passed. The landlord sold the town house in which we lived and we moved to our lovely cottage in the woods, high up in the mountains. There were no other houses nearby, only the tents of the Kazakh shepherds. We were as free as birds. The horses, the cow and Ishka were all happy at the change. They spent their days grazing in the mountain meadows and drinking the clear water from the springs.

We did not ride Ishka now, for she was expecting another foal.

One day we were leading her through a Kazakh shepherds' camp, about half an hour's climb up the mountain from our cottage. Yakub, an old one-eyed shepherd, called us over, took a look at Ishka and said with a smile:

"She have baby soon."

"How soon?"

"Who knows? May have today, may have to-morrow."

"Please, Yakub, won't you help her? We're afraid we won't know when she'll have her baby. She killed her other one."

"Give three rubles. I take care."

We looked at each other unhappily.

"We don't have three rubles," we said and set off again.

"Hey, you! Girls! Come back. All right. I take care. Only, you know, you get me sugar, you get me tea, you get me tobacco, you get me little bit everything when nobody looks."

We were overjoyed and thanked Yakub heartily. When we got home we began "getting everything".

Yakub tied Ishka up near his tent. He brought out a felt mat, spread it on a stone in the sun, sprawled on it and accepted our gifts. Ishka did not have her foal that night or the next night, either. In the daytime Yakub would lie in the sun near Ishka, while we showered him with gifts. At night he took Ishka into his tent. Those two days happened to be holidays. Mother was baking meat pies at home, but none of us ate a single one. We promptly carried off everything we were given and handed it over to Yakub. Soon we had taken all our treasures to the big white rock near the tent.

"This what?" Yakub asked, holding up a celluloid doll. "This no good. Get more tea."

We were managing our raids on the tea caddy, the sugar bin and Father's tobacco quite nicely, but we were faced with a real problem when Yakub demanded a shirt and trousers. We searched through the house in vain.

7-911

"Mother, don't we have a spare shirt and trousers anywhere?"

"What do you need them for?"

"For something."

"Tell me why you want them and I'll look for some."

But Yakub had made us promise faithfully that we would not breathe a word about our arrangement to our parents and so we said nothing.

"Isn't there a single miserable old shirt and trousers in the whole house for your very own children?" I cried, choosing a convenient moment when Father was alone in the room.

"And what could they be needing a 'miserable old shirt and trousers' for?"

"We need them."

Father rummaged about in his knapsack and came up with two shirts.

"But there aren't any trousers," he said. "Perhaps our very own children will be able to get along without them?"

We took the shirts and set out for Yakub's tent. He was still lying outside in the sun. Ishka was standing nearby with a tiny little grey donkey beside her.

Though its legs were still wobbly, it was already trying to play and kick. Ishka's eyes never left her baby. She licked it, nursed it and guarded it jealously.

"Is a girl, a little girl donkey," Yakub said.

"How wonderful! But what shall we call her? We can't call her Ishka."

"Milka, milaya!* You're all mine! You're as fuzzy as a chick!" Natasha cried in ecstasy as she gently patted the baby's soft leg.

"Milka, Milka," we all chanted.

Yakub tied a rope around Ishka's neck and led her down towards the cottage. The tiny new-born foal jerked its head and trotted off after its mother, stumbling over its own wobbly legs.

"Thank you, Yakub," Mother said and gave the shepherd a ruble.

Father had guessed where his shirts had gone to, and after some searching he came up with a pair of trousers as well.

We played with Milka as if she were a doll. Indeed, she was just like a toy. She was an exact copy of Ishka, except that she was unbelievably tiny. The very next morning she was prancing about, poking her pretty little head close to the dogs and kicking out at them angrily when they growled at her.

We saw our chance when Milka had had her fill of milk and was hopping about in the sun. We scooped her up and ran into the house.

Ishka looked around, brayed loudly and began galloping round and round the house, looking in at

---

* Milaya, milka (Russ.)—sweetie.

every window. Meanwhile, Milka was exploring the room. She rubbed her soft nose against our hands, wiggled her ears and gazed at the beds, the chairs and our toys.

Suddenly Ishka stuck her head in through the window. Her braying was more like a wail as she tried to climb in.

"Let's open the door for her," Sonya said. She went to the door and called Ishka.

In the meantime we had thought up some more mischief. We put a skirt on Milka, stuck her front legs through the sleeves of a blouse and tied a kerchief round her head.

"What a lovely little girl she is!"

Milka was a scream. She looked just like a monkey.

Then we heard Ishka's hoofs on the porch. She rushed in, looked wildly round the room, saw Milka on my lap and screeched with terror. We could practically hear her screaming: "My goodness! Look what they've done to the child!"

I set Milka down. She hobbled over to her mother, getting her feet all tangled in the skirt. Ishka grabbed hold of it with her teeth and pulled. She was trembling and breathing heavily from all the excitement, and her gasps sounded like, "Oh, oh, oh!"

We helped her undress Milka and she finally led her outside.

"Will someone please tell me what kind of an animal this is! Does she look at all like a donkey?"

Mother would ask as she kept stumbling over Milka in every room of the house. "She must think she's a dog. Why is she forever underfoot?"

We did not know who Milka thought she was, but she really did spend most of the time with us in the house, near the house, or in the mountains and did not play with the other animals at all. We spoiled her so terribly that when she got bigger and it was time to break her into a harness she was already a capricious, unruly creature.

She was intelligent and quickly learned all the simple commands. But there were times when she did not want to obey any of them.

"You should teach her a lesson once and for all," Yulia said to Natasha. "Wait and see. You'll have your hands full later on."

But Natasha was not firm enough. Besides, Milka knew that her little mistress always had a lump of sugar or something just as tasty tucked away in her pocket. That is why she probably never paid much attention to Natasha's threats or punishment.

Milka trotted faster and better than Ishka, but she had a thousand different twists and turns and we kept falling off her. Everyone preferred to ride Ishka, for with each passing year she was becoming more and more docile.

Natasha was the only one who dared ride Milka. She would often rub a bruised spot but never liked to mention it.

"Maybe I did it on purpose. Maybe I just wanted to jump off when she was galloping," she would say.

Now that we had two donkeys we would spend our days journeying up and down the mountains and through the forest. When someone asked Father where we were, he would go out on the porch and train his field-glasses on the mountains. There, high up on the ridge of a mountain or on a slope were two little donkeys climbing like goats with bright flashes of cotton dresses in between.

"There they are, those rascals! Look how high they've climbed! I don't know how they haven't broken their necks yet. One of these days I'll have to take those donkeys away from them!"

"We'll have to sell the donkeys in the autumn," Father said one day.

"Why?"

"We won't have enough hay for all the animals, and you had better be thinking of school in the winter, not donkeys."

"Well, we don't need your hay! We'll put away all the fodder we need for Ishka and Milka ourselves."

"I'd like to see how you're going to do that."

"You will."

Now we put all our energy into storing up hay for the winter, for Ishka and Milka were at stake.

At sunrise we would head for the mountains. There we would pull up grass all day long, stuff it into the large sacks we had brought along, cart it home and spread it out on the roof of the barn to dry. Our hands soon became covered with huge blisters, which made pulling up grass very painful. Then Sonya found a rusty old scythe. It took a lot of scheming to get it sharpened without being discovered.

As usual, we set off for the mountains early in the morning. Sonya rode the big mare, Mashka, I rode the old pacer, while Yulia and Natasha rode the donkeys.

When we got to the meadow we dismounted, hobbled the horses and got down to work. Sonya swung the scythe expertly. She cut off a huge clump of grass and the sole of her sandal as well.

While we were gazing sadly at her sandal, Yulia picked up the scythe and began to work. She seemed to be doing nicely.

"Just look at her!"

Suddenly, she cried out and dropped the scythe. Her hand was bleeding.

I grabbed our bottle of drinking water, wet my handkerchief and held it to the cut. The bleeding gradually stopped.

"You can't work till your hand heals. So you'd better stay here at the edge of the meadow and cook our potatoes. You can keep an eye on the house, and if anyone calls us you can tell us. Father was angry again yesterday because we never hear him when he calls."

"All right. You make a fire and start it going and I'll keep adding wood to it."

We made a fire at the edge of a small grove. Then we set the pot to boil and went off to pull up more grass. We did not take the scythe, for we decided there was something wrong with it. When we went back to the grove for lunch we had just barely managed to fill one sack. The potatoes were cooked, but cold.

"That's all right. Hot potatoes taste awful in such heat."

We stretched out on a blanket under the trees. It was very still. For some strange reason it is always very still in the mountains at midday. You could smell the nectar in the air, some birds were singing, twigs snapped here and there and from below came the low rumbling of the river. Yulia went to the edge of the grove to have a look at the house.

"Someone's come to visit us and everyone has gone to meet them," she called.

We all joined her. The house looked like a toy. Several people on horseback rode up to the porch. Tiny figures were bustling about.

"Hurry, let's go home," Sonya said. "Maybe they've brought another animal."

By the time I mounted my horse Sonya was zigzagging downhill. Yulia started after her, slipping down Ishka's neck the whole time and giving her great blows on the jaw which forced the donkey to turn from side to side.

I headed straight down to save time and naturally slid right up to the horse's ears. He lowered his head and shook me off gently, so that I landed at his feet.

When my first shock of surprise was over I turned quickly to see if my sisters had noticed, but Sonya and Yulia were intent on riding down the hill and were paying no attention to me. Natasha was still fussing with Milka up on the meadow. She had seen what had happened and was laughing as she noticed my embarrassment.

Then she untied Milka and mounted her. Milka, unmindful of Natasha, galloped straight down the mountain trying to catch up with Ishka.

Natasha's laughter froze as she whizzed past me. She was clutching Milka's back for dear life, trying her best to hang on. Milka flew on excitedly. She overtook Ishka and the mare. At the very foot of the mountain she suddenly turned sharply, lowered her head and kicked up her legs.

We all saw a little red pinafore and two bare feet fly helplessly through the air.

Natasha rolled head over heels down the hill and disappeared in a clump of bushes. Milka, still kicking out wildly, galloped off towards the house.

We ran down and found Natasha sitting gloomily beside a large rock. There were two light streaks on her dusty face. The tears had already dried, and Natasha hoped we would not notice that she had been crying.

We all pretended we did not.

"Good for you, Natasha," said Sonya. "I thought we'd find you crying your eyes out."

"Those old donkeys!" Natasha grumbled. "You just keep sliding off them!"

"Didn't I warn you about spoiling Milka?" Yulia said primly. "Ishka isn't too obedient, either, but still.... You know, it hurts when you fall off her, too," she added quite sincerely.

"What I can't understand is that we keep falling off horses, but it never bothers us!" I said. "You just get a little bump and you get up. But here...."

"That's because horses are so tall. The wind holds you up while you're falling, but when you fall off a donkey you're closer to the ground."

"That doesn't sound right. If that's the case, it's better to fall off the roof than off a chair."

"That's not it at all," Natasha said, getting up with an effort. We guessed that she had fallen on the rock. "That's not it at all."

She never did explain what she meant, but limped off towards the house.

But we all understood that what she had really wanted to say was: "It's just that Milka is such a mean, ungrateful creature."

Our sore, blistered hands made us put off our "mowing" for several days. We raked the dry hay and stacked it.

The donkeys' food for the winter was increasing daily. We now had a large haystack of dry hay and half a haystack that was still drying.

But those awful blisters were ruining everything! The weather was fine, yet the days were slipping away.

It was the middle of September. The days were getting cooler and the nights were getting cold.

A chill wind blew from the glaciers, though the sun was still hot and the days were wonderful.

Autumn had already come to the forest. The ashberries and hawthorns were bright red, the beech trees were yellow, the curly wild hops hung in tangled bunches.

Our parents saw we had been idling away our time for several days.

"Why don't you get me some hops for the winter?" Mother said. "I'll bake some meat pies tomorrow and you can take them along when you go to pick the hops."

We set out early the next morning. The hops grew farther upstream and so we decided to take along a butterfly net to catch some fish on the way.

"But please don't break your necks," were the usual words of farewell from our parents.

The path was steep and stony. Jumping from rock to rock with the donkeys' hoofs clattering on the stones, we started happily up the mountain, singing a marching song.

We were lucky to find a good place. There were hops growing everywhere. We tied a long rope to Ishka and set her out to graze as we climbed the trees that were hung with the beautiful vines.

"I've found a wonderful bush! Look how many hops there are here!"

"So have I! Come over here!"

"Look at that one over there! We'll get a whole bagful in an hour!"

At first, we kept on talking, but soon fell silent, each too busy picking hops. The vines gave off a strong, stifling odour. I felt my hands growing limp. It was as if someone had put a heavy pillow on my head. Then I stopped picking and looked around. To the left and right of me my sisters were swinging in the branches. Their hands also seemed to be moving very slowly.

I was just about to ask them if they didn't feel as I did when suddenly the branch Yulia was sitting on sprang upwards.

"Yulia fell into the bushes!" I shouted, shaking off my drowsiness with an effort.

We climbed down and made our way to the place where Yulia had fallen. She was lying on the ground. She looked very sleepy.

"Yulia! Yulia! Get up!" we shouted, shaking her.

She struggled to her feet and we led her out of the bushes.

"Let's run back to camp! Let's get out of here!"

We ran across the clearing and down to the river and began splashing water on our faces.

"Let's go swimming!"

"Let's! First we'll have a swim, then we'll catch some fish, then we'll cook some chowder and then we'll finish picking those awful hops."

"It made me nauseous," Yulia said. She threw off her clothes and was the first one in.

We swam and splashed until we were blue and our teeth began to chatter. Then we waded up and down the stream, slipping and scratching our bare feet on the stones, poking our nets under the big rocks and into the hollows. In all, we caught five tiny fish.

We made a fire on the bank and cooked our chowder, adding onions and potatoes to it. When it was done we gulped it down greedily, dipping our spoons right into the pot. As we ate we carried on a most interesting scientific discussion. The topic was: Why did Ishka always stick her tail out when she brayed?

"I wonder if you've noticed that if you press her tail down, she'll stop braying."

"I guess she doesn't have enough air left."

"I wonder if Milka will be the same way."

Just then we heard a terrible howl. We jumped up and listened. It was Ishka.

"Something's happened! Hurry! Run!"

Milka had been wandering about high above us, while Ishka had been tied up. She had brayed because

109

she had wanted to follow Milka, but instead she had got tangled in her rope and had rolled downhill. The rope had tightened around her neck like a noose.

As we came running up we saw her hanging over a ditch, slowly choking to death. Her tongue was hanging out of her foaming mouth, her legs were kicking wildly as she gasped for air. We tried frantically to loosen the knot but only succeeded in tightening the noose.

"What'll we do? Oh, dear! What'll we do?"

Sonya was holding Ishka's head, while Yulia and I were trying our best to untie the rope, but it was no use. Ishka was dying in our arms.

And then, suddenly....

Natasha shouted:

"My knife! I have a knife! Here it is!"

She had been cutting onions and still had the knife in her hand, but the sight of Ishka had paralysed us all and no one had noticed it.

"Give it to me! Hurry! Hold the rope!"

With shaking hands we began hacking away at the heavy rope. The knife was dull, it sawed instead of cutting.

"Press harder! Harder!"

The knife squeaked as it bit into the rope. Yulia and Natasha bent over it, watching its movements.

Finally, the knot was loosened. Ishka dropped her head to the grass and took a deep breath.

For several minutes she lay there motionless. Then she shook her head, jumped to her feet, turned around and looked for Milka.

"*Hee-haw! Hee-haw!*" Ishka brayed in a deep bass voice with her tail standing straight out.

"*Hee-haw! Hee-haw!*" Milka answered.

Her mischievous head, wreathed in hops, popped out high up the hill.

"*Hee-haw! Hee-haw!*" the canyon echoed joyously.

VASKA

We were playing in the orchard behind the house
when the hunters returned. Someone shouted from
the porch:

"Run! Hurry! See what they've got!"

We all ran to look.

Several wagons were rolling through the yard. They
were piled high with animal skins, the horns of
mountain goats and carcasses of boars. Father was
walking alongside the last wagon. A tiger-cub was
hunched up near the driver's seat, looking around
warily. Yes, it was a real, live tiger-cub! He was tired
and dusty, his claws were sunk into the side of the
wagon as it bumped across the yard. When the horse
finally stopped near the tiny crowd of people waiting
by the porch he became frightened, backed away and
looked at Father helplessly.

"Well, Vaska, we're home at last," Father said.

He picked the cub up and carried it to the porch.

A tiger-cub was such an unusual visitor that we, too, felt lost.

"Don't bring him up here!" Natasha shouted. "My toys are here."

"Tigers don't eat toys," said Yulia. She paused and added, "We'll have to treat him very well, or he might start biting."

"He's not a pussy-cat, you know."

"Look how huge his eyes are. And his tail. Did you notice his tail? It's just dragging along the ground."

"That's not true! You always make things up."

"Let's go and see!"

We ran up the steps, jostling each other in our haste. The cub was pacing up and down, sniffing at everything intently. After the long bumpy ride he was probably still dizzy and thought the floor was swaying. He stumbled about as if he were drunk and would sit down suddenly and close his eyes. But the moment he felt better he would start sniffing again, as if that were a job he just had to do.

A padded jacket was thrown over the railing with one of the sleeves hanging down. Vaska smacked it with his paw and pulled it towards him. Sonya laughed. He raised his head and stared at her.

Now at last we could get a good look at him. He was about the size of a six-month-old St. Bernard puppy with a large broad head, round green eyes and short ears. His front paws were heavy and powerful, but his hind paws were much thinner. He had a thin, bony body and his tail was as long as a snake.

"Why, he's still a baby," Natasha said.

He was clumsy, small and lonely and he pressed against Father's leg and rubbed up and down it, as if to say: "I'm a stranger here and I'm still very small, so please don't let anyone hurt me."

While Father was busy unhitching the horses, unpacking his things and washing up after the journey, we picked the cub up, carried him into the house and put him on the couch, the place of honour.

We tried to find something unusual about him and examined him closely. Then we fed him some fresh warm milk from a little bowl. After he had had his fill he stretched out on the couch and squinted at the lamp. Though he was very tired, he did not fall asleep, but kept twitching his ears.

When the table was set for supper and Father came into the room the tiger raised his head and leaned towards him, making a strange sound like loud purring.

"Did you hear that? He's so happy he's laughing," Natasha cried.

Father patted the tiger. Then Vaska stretched out on the couch again and fell soundly asleep while we talked on and on.

During supper Father told us all about him. He had

been caught some 400 miles from our town, in the bulrushes near a large lake called Balkhash. A Kazakh hunter who was a very good friend of Father's had tracked down the pair of two tigers. There were no tigers in those parts, but this pair had come across from Persia. The hunter notified Father and continued his watch. He discovered that the tigers had not come to hunt, but to hide, for the tigress would soon have cubs.

A short while later the tigress disappeared. Then the tiger went back across the mountain pass and never returned.

As the hunter was expecting Father to arrive any day, he had crossed and recrossed the countryside, searching for the tigress; finally he had come upon fresh tracks in the sand which led down to a river.

The hunter hid in the bushes and scanned the bulrushes growing along the banks. He saw the tigress on the other side. She was creeping through the thicket, carrying something heavy in her teeth. Suddenly, she dropped her burden, swam across the river, trotted past the hunter and was about to disappear. The old hunter knew what was up. He got on his little horse, but instead of pursuing the tigress, he galloped towards the place where she had dropped whatever it was she had been carrying.

He had guessed correctly: there, huddled close together in the thick reeds, were two tiny cubs.

The hunter picked them up, shoved them into two bags and mounted his horse. The cubs squealed and fought and kept crawling out of the bags. But the hunter only pressed them closer with his knees and urged on his horse.

He knew the danger he faced, for if the tigress followed him, she would easily catch up with his tired old horse and kill it and the cub-snatcher as well. His rusty old gun was not of much use: the barrel had come loose and was tied to the stock with a piece of rag.

And so the fearless hunter had risked kidnapping a pair of tiger-cubs with nothing more to protect him than his faithful nag and a useless gun.

As he approached the village he began thinking frantically of a way to escape the tigress' wrath. Luckily, Father and the other hunters arrived just then.

When Father discovered the terrible danger his friend had braved, he took his own wonderful gun and presented it to him. The Kazakh hunter was very touched and gave one of the cubs to Father in return.

The journey from the distant village to our house was a long and difficult one for Vaska. They travelled nearly half the way by camel caravan. Poor Vaska was sick from the swaying movement and kept throwing up. At such times Father would get off his camel and carry Vaska awhile.

This is how their friendship began.

"Vaska really had a hard time of it," Father concluded. "Once I really got scared. I thought he was done for. He was lying on the ground with his eyes rolling and his legs twitching. It looked like the end had come. But he got his breath back and was all right again."

"I don't see why he shouldn't have got his breath back," one of the hunters interrupted. "We had to spend a whole week in Fishermen's Village because of him, and we looked after him as well as if he had been the Sultan of Turkey."

We all laughed.

"Why aren't you asleep yet?" Mother suddenly exclaimed. "My goodness! It's twelve o'clock! I want you all in bed in a minute."

As we drifted out of the room each of us patted Vaska's tail respectfully. It lay proudly across the bolster.

Meanwhile, our parents began discussing where they would put the cub for the night. Mother did not know Vaska at the time and was afraid to let him loose, while Father said that he was tamer than a kitten and it was silly to be afraid of him. At any rate, they could always leave him where he was and close the door.

That is exactly what they did. They left Vaska sleeping on the couch, turned off the lamp and locked the door.

The moment the key turned in the lock Vaska raised

his head. He saw that everything was dark and deserted.

And then the "fierce" tiger jumped off the couch and raced around the room, bumping into all the furniture and yowling with fright.

Father thought that he would stop after a while, but he did not. At first, his voice sounded angry. Then his howling became more and more pitiful. Finally, Father unlocked the door. Vaska was so happy to see him that he rushed up and began licking Father's feet. Naturally, it all ended with him being taken into our parents' bedroom, where he was put on a long thin chain and left to sleep on a felt mat under the sewing-machine table. Vaska looked very happy as he curled up on his blanket.

While Mother was brushing her hair and talking to Father Vaska was very still, but the moment Father left the room he jumped up and began whimpering anxiously.

When Father came back he patted Vaska and everyone fell asleep at last.

Natasha's first words the next morning were:

"Was the tiger-cub Vaska real or make-believe?"

She had been dreaming of a tiger-cub all night and couldn't quite tell what part had been the dream and what part had been real.

"He certainly was real," Sonya replied and we all went into the dining room to see if yesterday's tiger-cub was still there.

The room was empty. We rushed to Mother's room. She pointed under the table and there he was, sitting up and staring at us out of his funny eyes.

We untied his chain and ran shouting and laughing to the orchard with Vaska in tow.

We raced about and introduced Vaska to our dogs, for we always invented games that included the dogs.

Vaska was very polite to them, but they seemed to sense what sort of a fellow he really was and ran off with their tails between their legs.

Our old hunting dog Zagrai was lying in the sun. Vaska walked over slowly and sniffed him. Zagrai rose lazily, took one look at Vaska and was gone in a flash.

The very smell of a tiger made the hunting dogs shiver. Mailik, a young mongrel, was the only one who knew nothing at all about hunting smells. He jumped over Vaska, crouched low, smacked him lightly with his paw, wagged his tail and barked loudly, inviting him to play.

Vaska perked up a bit and lumbered after Mailik.

We had cleaned the house and finished our chores and were going to have tea, after which we intended to feed Vaska.

But he would have none of it. He jumped up on the couch, sniffed loudly and decided that the tasty smells were coming from the table. In a flash he was on someone's lap, sweeping all the cups and saucers into a pile in front of him and growling fiercely.

We all became frightened and jumped up. Father raised his hand and shouted: "Down! Where's my strap?" But he had met his match. Vaska only growled louder. We thought this was great fun. Vaska was a fine fellow, he wasn't afraid of anyone. He could stand up for himself. We begged Father to give in and feed Vaska first. But our parents were afraid that if they gave in once they would never be able to manage him afterwards. Father grabbed Vaska by the scruff of his neck and threw him out of the window.

The outside door was shut.

Vaska began rattling the door, growling quietly at first, then more fiercely.

He growled and banged so loud and long that we finally had to give in and open the door.

Vaska flew into the room, grabbed his bowl from Mother's hands, stuck his head into it and gobbled up the raw eggs she had given him. Then he had some milk. He lapped it up, licked his chops and stretched out on the couch. Now, when he had had his fill, he could calmly watch others eating.

After that, we always fed him first and then sat down to our meals.

In this way Vaska proved that though he was still very small, he wasn't an ordinary creature, but a tiger, and we would have to seriously consider his likes and dislikes.

Several days passed. We were so used to Vaska we felt as though he had always been with us.

And how good-natured he was! He never annoyed anyone, he was never underfoot, he was never in the way. Vaska spent his days playing in the orchard, making his rounds of the yard, the stable and all the nooks and crannies. Whenever he felt tired he would come into the dining room, stretch out on the couch and have a nap.

We fed Vaska very well. Everyone remembered how mean he could be when he was hungry, and he knew exactly at what time he was to be fed. Often we would just be cracking raw eggs into his bowl or pouring out his milk when he would come bouncing in from the orchard.

"Shame on you, Natasha. Even Vaska can tell the time, but you can't seem to learn at all," we teased.

Besides the raw eggs and milk which Vaska had for breakfast and supper, he had the same dinner we did.

It was so funny to watch him eat soup and dumplings! First, he would fish out all the dumplings and lay them in a row on the floor beside his bowl; then he would lap up the soup. Finally, for dessert, he would eat one dumpling at a time.

When Vaska was eating he became ferocious. He would lie down on the floor with his front paws on either side of his bowl and no one ever dared come near him then! Once my sister went over to move his dish. Vaska growled into the bowl, choked on a piece of food and smacked her smartly with his heavy paw.

The dogs were more cautious than we were and never dared go near him when he was eating. Mailik, the one who had played with him the very first morning, was the only one who had the courage to stick his nose into Vaska's bowl. And though Vaska growled, he never chased him away.

It was only while he was eating, or if someone slapped his stomach or touched his tail, that Vaska flew into a rage and would bite anyone within biting distance. He considered his stomach and his tail two sacred and untouchable parts of his body.

Once someone called to us from the yard. We stuck our heads out of the window. Vaska put his front paws on the window-sill and looked out, too. In the commotion Sonya stepped on his tail. He spun around and snapped at her leg. It began to bleed. Sonya was frightened. But the moment she lifted her foot from his precious tail, Vaska forgot his anger. He began licking her leg as if he were trying to apologise.

When people say that tigers become vicious at the smell of blood, do not believe them. You should have seen Vaska: he never dreamed of being vicious. He licked Sonya's wound as though he realised it was wrong to snap at other people's legs.

Once, as Vaska was strolling up and down the porch, he caught sight of a broom. He crept up to it and pounced. Then he galloped off to the orchard, shaking it and dragging it along. When he returned a while later, two or three straws in his mouth were all that remained of the broom.

We laughed at him, teased him and soon forgot all about the incident. But then, two days later, he chewed up another broom, and then a third. It was becoming a bad habit. He just couldn't pass a broom without pouncing on it and tearing it to bits. It seemed to us that his expression was especially mean at such times, as if he were getting even with all the brooms in the world.

And this is exactly what he was doing.

On the long journey to our house Father had stopped off to rest at a friend's place on the way. The man was a hunter. He had a very stern wife. She would hit Vaska with her broom whenever he left dirty paw-marks on her clean rugs. That was when Vaska learned to hate every broom in the world. It was then also that he discovered the difference between a woman's skirt and a man's boots. When the angry woman (a human in a skirt, as far as he was concerned) chased after him with her broom, he ran to seek protection from people who wore boots. These were Father and his friend. They would always shield him. From then on he had a special love for boots, while he never really did get used to skirts. Mother fed Vaska and spent the most time with him. We could see that he preferred her to all the other women, though he couldn't stand her skirts and had chewed on most of them.

Vaska had a very keen sense of smell. For instance, he could not stand the smell of perfume of flowers. If he happened to smell a flower in the garden by accident, he would wrinkle up his nose and sneeze for a long while afterwards. He could smell a sausage from a great distance and apparently thought it was the most wonderful smell in the world.

At the slightest whiff of sausage he would become terribly excited and would begin to yelp plaintively. He was just like a spoiled child, whining: "Where's the sausage? I want some sausage! Give me my sausage!"

One evening we were having sausages for supper. Vaska, who had just had his supper, was in the next room. He came bounding into the dining room and climbed right up on the table.

"No, you don't!" Father said. "You've had your supper. Off to bed with you!" And he threw Vaska on the couch. Then he put the sausages up on a high shelf of the cupboard.

But Vaska was too excited to hear him. He put his front paws on the table, saw that there were no sausages there and raced around the room in a frenzy with his nose in the air. Finally, he had an idea. He jumped on the window-sill and began sniffing. Then he ran over to the cupboard and began throwing himself against it, growling angrily.

"Do you think he'll reach them? Maybe he'll give up after a while."

Vaska was going mad right in front of us. He scratched and chewed a corner of the cupboard and each time he sprang on it he fell back like a sack of potatoes.

Finally, when he was completely furious, he climbed up on the table again and was about to leap at the cupboard from there.

"We might as well give him a piece," we finally decided.

Father cut off a piece of sausage and said: "Here, catch, Vaska!"

Vaska was still standing on the table. He opened his mouth wide. The sausage flew right into it and disappeared in a flash. But Vaska still stood there, staring at us, as if to say: "What sort of monkey-business is this? What happened to that sausage? Hm?"

I remember a very boring, gloomy Sunday. It rained all day and there was a cold wind blowing. We wandered aimlessly from room to room, and everyone felt chilly.

"Let's make a fire and roast some dry corn," Sonya said.

Everyone was excited with the project. There was a great commotion as we ran for kindling and started chopping a block of wood into chips. My sister and I went up to the attic where we kept our strings of dry corn. We brought in the firewood and began building a fire. The stove was opposite the couch where Vaska was now lying with his head on the bolster.

He watched intently as a match burst into flame, chips caught fire and the wood began to burn and crackle. He pricked up his ears and sat up in surprise. My, my! How interesting!

We were chattering excitedly and did not see him slip off the couch.

Suddenly we heard a loud *wuffff!!!*

There was Vaska. He had stuck his head into the firebox and had gasped from fright. This had made the flames leap up and poor Vaska became petrified.

Luckily, Father was in the room. He rushed over and pulled Vaska away by the tail.

Vaska's whiskers and eyebrows were charred, his muzzle was full of ashes. He curled up in a corner of the couch and looked at us, so lost and pitiful, that we thought he would burst into tears any moment.

That's one way to find out what a stove is all about!

"Hurry, girls, come here!" Yulia called in between giggles.

We rushed to the porch.

"What's the matter?"

Yulia covered her mouth with her hand and shook a finger at us. "Shh! Look! Over there. See Vaska?"

There, sitting on the top step of the porch, was Pavlik, the neighbour's four-year-old son. He was crying and mumbling in a hurt voice as he tried to push Vaska away. But Vaska was paying no attention to him. He was standing on his hind paws with his front paws on Pavlik's shoulders and was busy "combing" Pavlik's hair. Vaska seemed awfully pleased and was purring gently.

What he was really doing was licking Pavlik's head, from the back of his neck to his forehead. The boy's hair was sticky and wet from saliva and stuck up like a brush. Vaska seemed to think this was very beautiful, and his eyes shone with pleasure.

"Let's chase him away! See how miserable Pavlik is."

"That's a fine barber for you, licking someone else's head!"

"He'd be smarter to lick his own belly or paws. He's not even doing a good job of it, because he's licking the wrong way."

Sonya went in to get a piece of sausage. She let Vaska smell it and tossed it across the porch.

When Vaska ran after it we rescued Pavlik.

Then Yulia poured some water from a big cup, I rubbed his sticky hair and Natasha held a jam tart which was to be his treat for all his suffering. Later, as he ate the tart, he explained what had happened:

"I was playing and he came up to me. He put his hands on my back over here," and he pointed to his shoulder, "and then he began smelling my head. And then he spit on my hair. I pushed him away and said: 'Go 'way, Vaska, I don't want to play.' But he laughed at me."

And Pavlik sobbed again, recalling Vaska's "brushing".

We tried to comfort him as best we could, but he looked so funny with his hair sticking up in all directions, his little jam-smeared face had such a hurt expression that we couldn't help laughing. When Pavlik saw that we were laughing he stopped crying and began to laugh, too. In time Pavlik finally got used to playing barber shop with Vaska. The same scene was often repeated, but now Pavlik never cried. Instead, he would be humming a little song or talking with Vaska and both of them would beam with contentment.

Vaska tried to "comb" us girls, but to no avail, for we had long hair that was always tightly braided and tied with ribbons, and we'd never let him get near enough to our heads to lick them.

Father sometimes let Vaska "comb" him. Often in the mornings he and Vaska would go into the orchard to play and wrestle. Vaska liked to grab Father's boot and drag it along. He would not leave Father alone for a minute and would really annoy him. When Father went into the orchard to read, Vaska would catch sight of him and follow stealthily, hiding in the bushes. No sooner would Father sit down and open his book than Vaska would come flying through the air in a tremendous leap, knocking the book from his hands. Snatching it up in his teeth, he would then head straight for the house in big funny jumps. However, Vaska was sometimes useful to us as well.

One day a travelling salesman came to the house and tried to talk Father into buying a folding cot, a contraption for pulling off boots, a specially designed knapsack and similar items.

Father was pressed for time, as he had a report to finish, and he did not know how to get rid of the annoying salesman. Then Vaska came bounding into Father's study. He had been looking for Father all over the house and had found him at last.

When the salesman saw Vaska he turned pale, his lips began to tremble.

"What's that?"

"That's kind of a cat. It's called a tiger," Father answered calmly.

"I guess I'd better be.... Uh.... Well, good-bye...."

The man gathered up his treasures hastily and was gone.

"Good boy! You really saved my neck this time," Father said.

Vaska was very unhappy when Father had to spend a week away from home.

He wandered about the house, stuck his head into the kitchen every now and then, sniffed at all of us and kept his ears cocked.

On the evening of the seventh day, when Vaska was chained to the table leg for the night, there was a sound of voices in the yard. Father had returned. Vaska rushed out to meet him, pulling the table across the room. It finally got stuck in the doorway. Then Father came hurrying over to Vaska.

How happy the cub was! He hugged Father's boots, licked them and purred as if he were laughing.

I don't remember who brought us our copy of *Uncle Tom's Cabin*, but for several days we forgot our games and would go off to the orchard in the morning to read. Sonya and I took turns reading aloud.

My younger sisters and the neighbours' boys would sit open-mouthed in a semicircle on the grass. When we came to Uncle Tom's death, the saddest part of the book, both the reader and the listeners wept bitterly.

Then someone leaned on Yulia's shoulder with a heavy sigh. Natasha, who was sitting opposite with tears streaming down her face, suddenly burst out laughing.

I caught my breath: had she gone mad with grief?

But she giggled wildly and pointed at Yulia.

Then we saw that Vaska had put his head on her shoulder. He was sighing sadly with his eyes closed, as if he, too, was sorry for Uncle Tom. Well, that was the end of our reading that day, for by then we were all rolling in the grass, shrieking with laughter.

Vaska had now been a member of the family for over a month. He had grown considerably and was stronger and more confident of himself. He was still clumsy, but sometimes, especially if he was stalking something, his movements became swift and graceful.

Vaska's coat was as shiny and smooth as velvet. It was reddish-gold with black stripes that reached to his light-grey stomach. By now Vaska was sleek and well-fed. It was a pleasure to look at him.

All day long he would be busy grooming himself, licking his paws and stomach, shaking himself to make himself still grander. At such times he was amazingly like a cat. Vaska was completely house-broken. He did have an accident once, but it was our fault, since we had forgotten to let him out. By the time we finally remembered, Vaska was terribly embarrassed and displeased, he crinkled up his nose and huffed loudly.

We untied him and he tore out into the orchard as fast as he could go. That day he bathed with special care.

Giving him a bath was quite an occasion.

A round hole had been specially dug in the orchard. It was about a yard deep and a yard across. The tiny stream that flowed nearby filled it with fresh water.

Mother would bring out a brush and a cake of soap, Father would bring a pail and, lastly, Vaska would appear, surrounded by a crowd of children.

Unlike all other cats, he loved to bathe.

First, Father would douse Vaska with water. Then Vaska was rubbed with green soap; after that he would climb into the hole by himself and stand there on his hind paws, holding out his front paws to Father. He was then scrubbed with a brush and rubbed, doused and rinsed, while he stood triumphantly in the hole, grunting with pleasure. When the bath was finally over, he would climb out of the hole, shake himself, roll around in the grass and cavort in the sunshine.

Vaska was a lot of bother and trouble, but he was growing into a really beautiful tiger.

He was not the least bit afraid of people. On the contrary, he always tried to attract their attention.

If we were all busy and paid no attention to him, he

seemed hurt because no one was patting him, scratching his ears, or talking to him.

Sometimes we purposely tried his patience.

For instance, we would all sit in a circle on the floor and begin to talk.

Vaska would come up and listen attentively. He was waiting for us to say, as we always did: "Ah, Vaska dear, here you are!" Then we were supposed to pat him.

But we made believe we did not notice him. He'd stand there listening for a while and then would touch one of our ribbons or the ties of our pinafores with his paw. But we'd keep right on talking, just as if he didn't exist.

Then he'd sit down in the circle with us, stare at us with wide, sad eyes, listen attentively and put in his own *aha!* whenever convenient.

That meant he was getting impatient at being ignored for so long.

We would laugh and say (but still not looking at him): "See how hard he's trying! Don't anyone say his name, or he'll guess we're talking about him and he won't feel bored any more."

We loved to tease him like that.

He tried to join in the conversation, to attract our attention in every possible way, and then, seeing that nothing helped, he would suddenly yawn loudly, opening his huge mouth wide.

His mouth was wonderful. It was red, with a sort of

fringe around it, and his teeth were huge and sharp.

We would forget our agreement, look down his throat and admire his teeth.

Then Vaska would feel he was again one of us. We would try to pry his mouth open a second time, but he would turn his head away happily, for he had made us notice him after all.

People from all over town and even from neighbouring villages and mountain hamlets came to see our tiger-cub. They would ring the bell outside the gate and we would run to open it.

"They say you have a tame tiger. Could we see him? We'll pay you for a look at him."

At first we were very excited about collecting kopecks from all these people. Once we even amassed two rubles, having charged five kopecks a head, but that made Father angry and he forbade us to take money. He did say, however, that they had to stand at a distance, that they could not pat Vaska and that no one was to give him anything to eat without permission.

We were very flattered to have grown-ups asking our permission about something.

"How many of you are there? All right. Stay right here outside the gate. We'll call him over, but don't try to pat him and don't give him anything to eat when he comes."

"All right. We'll do exactly as you say."

Then they would line up near the gate.

We would go into the orchard and call Vaska. When he came out to the visitors he always looked very important.

At the sight of him they would stumble backwards, making him look at us in surprise.

We would then calm them by saying:

"There's nothing to be afraid of. He's quite tame."

"He doesn't even know why you're so frightened. See how nice he is."

At this, we would put our hands in his mouth, pat his head, scratch his ears and his neck, lift his heavy paw and show the pads to the visitors.

"See," we would say, "he's pulled his claws in. There's nothing to be afraid of."

They would look at Vaska and the more they looked, the more they wanted to look. They would take such a liking to him that they felt they just had to pat him.

"No," we'd say. "We can't let you pat him, because that will get us in trouble."

"No, it won't".

"Yes, it will."

But they kept insisting, until we'd finally say:

"Well, he's a tiger, after all. What if he sinks his teeth into you? What'll we do then?"

They usually stopped wanting to pat him after that.

Once, when Vaska was strolling about the orchard, he noticed a hole in the fence. He stuck his head through it and saw a street with dogs running up and down, carters and horses, and children playing ball in the distance. Some men were playing cards on the grass near the fence.

Vaska took it all in. Then he pulled his head back, snorted and said *wuff!* excitedly.

He stuck his head through the hole again.

Since he could never stand to be ignored by humans he watched the men for a while, and finally crawled through the hole and came up to them.

The card players turned around and saw him.

"*Aha!*" said Vaska.

They jumped to their feet. One man said to another:

"Come on, Vaska! Let's get out of here! That's the forester's tiger. He's a mean thing if ever I saw one."

Since he had said: "Come on, Vaska!" the tiger decided he had been speaking to him, so he followed them. The men became terrified and broke into a run, while a woman passing nearby shrieked. Vaska became confused. He sat down in the dust in the middle of the road and began scratching his ear. Just then Father happened to walk over to the fence. He looked out and saw Vaska sitting there, scratching his ear thoughtfully, while a group of neighbours were watching him from a distance and laughing.

Father climbed over the fence and was about to lead Vaska home. However, at the sight of him the neighbours took courage and said:

"Wait a bit! Don't lead him away yet."

"Isn't he interesting?"

"Is he a cat or some other kind of animal?"

Father told them all about tigers and then showed them how Vaska could wrestle. He slapped him gently on the jaws and Vaska tried to fend his hand off with his paw and slap Father in return.

When Father finally led him off, the neighbours followed at a distance.

"Good for you, Vaska!" they said. "Thank you for coming out to see us!"

We had many chickens and Vaska took a great interest in them.

One day he went for a walk in the yard after the rain. There were puddles everywhere. Vaska walked around them carefully, shaking his paws like a cat.

Suddenly, he noticed a hen and her chicks pecking in the sunshine. The little chicks were like balls of fluff. Vaska pressed his ears close to his head (he always did that when he was stalking prey) and flattened himself close to the ground, ready to spring at the chicks.

The hen sensed the terrible danger and became worried. Collecting her chicks, she fluffed out her feathers as threateningly as she could and attacked Vaska furiously, flapping her wings, jumping at him, trying to peck out his eyes.

Vaska became frightened. He shook his head and took to his heels. He didn't see where he was going and raced straight through the puddles, raising sprays

138

of muddy water. The hen was right behind him; her attacks were getting bolder and bolder as she pecked at him from behind. It was not until Vaska came scrambling up the porch steps in terror that she turned around, flapped her wings and headed proudly towards her chicks.

Vaska's next encounter with the hens was on the eve of a big holiday. Everyone was very busy that day. We had been cleaning and cooking since early morning and in the confusion had forgotten to feed the animals.

The dogs were hungry. So was Vaska.

Suddenly, Sonya burst into the kitchen, shouting:

"Mother! Come and see what the dogs have done!"

"What's the matter?" she said, hurrying off after Sonya.

The dogs had decided to see to their meals themselves and had begun by wolfing down the ham that was intended for our holiday dinner. They had broken into the cellar and made off with it.

We suddenly remembered that Vaska had not been fed, either, and rushed to get his food ready. But it was too late. Vaska had been sitting in the sunshine in the yard, hungry and cross, frowning at the hens that were scratching about. He could not muster up the courage to come close to them, for he still remembered the pecking he had got.

Just then a lame rooster hobbled by.

Vaska pounced, and in a second the unfortunate bird was in his teeth. We had seen it happen from where we stood on the porch and had shouted and screamed at him.

Father came running out of the house. He grabbed the first stick he saw, smacked Vaska sharply and shouted:

"Put him down! Put him down this minute!"

Vaska growled menacingly through clenched teeth. His eyes were blazing and he really looked terrifying. Father realised that if he let him get away with it this time, it would soon happen again.

He smacked him a second time.

Vaska was growling wildly and hopping about, but he wouldn't let go of the rooster.

Then Father picked him up by his hind paws and swung him against the fence, rooster and all.

True, it was a cruel punishment, but it calmed the raging tiger down immediately. He dropped the strangled rooster and sat there limply with a stunned look on his face.

Mother fed him soon after and he slunk off to the orchard.

It took him a long time to forgive Father. He would not go near him or rub against him or even "talk" to him.

But he never touched another chicken. True, sometimes he would pounce on them from his hiding place in the bushes, but this was only a game which usually ended with the chickens squawking wildly as they scattered, while Vaska, frightened by his own mischief, fled in the opposite direction.

All four of us sisters had managed to come into the world in such a way that our birthdays were in close succession.

You are supposed to have a cake for your birthday and company, and there has to be a lot of noise and laughter all evening, and then, of course, there is the very special present. One birthday isn't too bad, but when you have to bake four birthday cakes in a row and have four evenings of noise and shrieking, it becomes a bit trying. By the time they were over, Mother was usually tired and cross and so we decided to combine our birthdays into one big celebration, but that day the cake and the company and the noise really had to be something!

On the eve of our combined birthday we all pitched in to help Mother. We swept the yard and the garden paths, and volunteered for the most difficult task, that of baking our big birthday cake. We were so concerned and anxious that we kept tasting the filling until only half of the necessary amount was left. Finally, Mother said:

"All right! That's enough help! I'll try and manage as best I can without you." With these words she sent us off to bed.

Later, when we were all sound asleep, she tiptoed into our room and put a present under each of our pillows. Then she went to bed herself.

The first thing we did next morning was to look under our pillows. Each of us found the thing we wished for most. Sonya had a big heavy volume of Brehm that was all about animals. I had a cardboard puppet theatre, Yulia had a big box of paints, and Natasha had a game called "Barnyard Animals".

We spread our presents out to admire them. Mother was just as happy as we were. She had come in for a minute to call us for breakfast but had remained in our room. In our excitement we forgot about breakfast completely.

Then, we had a visitor. The porch door was open and no one heard him come into the dining room. It was one of Father's clerks. He went over to the table and admired our birthday cake and the inscription on it, which read: "Happy Birthday, Dears!"

"Oh, so they're having a party today," he said to himself and walked up and down the room, humming a song.

The visitor was a small, thin man, no taller than a ten-year-old boy. However, he was so straight and stiff and looked so pompous that no one would ever have treated him lightly.

He usually greeted children by offering them two fingers and raising his eyebrows arrogantly. We did not like him and made fun of him on the sly.

As he walked up and down the room he pulled out his handkerchief and smoothed his moustache. A strong smell of cologne filled the room.

Suddenly, someone standing quite close to him said *phew!* disgustedly.

He looked around and wondered who it could be.

It was Vaska. The strong smell had made him sneeze. He sat up on the couch, where he had been sleeping, and sniffed again. It really was disgusting. He made an awful face. His tongue hung out and the skin all around his nose was wrinkled. Now the poor man was completely at a loss. After all, this was no laughing matter! There, sitting not two feet away from him, was a real, live tiger. A tiger, mind you, and it was making horrible faces at him!

Vaska sneezed again and shook his head.

A wild animal never understands why people smell so strongly. Animals always try to have as little smell as possible, to keep their enemies from discovering them.

The man was thinking frantically of a way to escape. He gazed mournfully at the open door but didn't dare budge.

Meanwhile, Vaska had an idea of his own. The strong-smelling "boy" had probably come to play with him. Vaska slipped off the couch, walked up to the man and grunted, as if to say: "All right, what'll we play?"

The man shuddered. Vaska backed away. He was beginning to have his doubts, for the "boy" was behaving strangely. He had a very strong smell, he shuddered and did not talk to Vaska as other people did. Indeed, he was behaving most strangely!

Vaska took one step back, then another. Finally he backed into the doorway and stood there.

"Nice kitty-kitty!" the man managed to squeak. "Run along now, pussy! Run along!"

And he waved his handkerchief. Vaska sneezed loudly again. The man darted around to the other side of the table.

Well! The "boy" had finally stopped acting funny and was ready to play. Vaska leaped happily after him. The man scrambled up on the couch with Vaska right behind. Then the man jumped on the table and crouched next to our birthday cake among the dishes.

144

For a moment Vaska couldn't understand what had happened to him.

That was a nice how-d'ye-do! They had just begun such a good game, and then the "boy" had disappeared.

Vaska rose up on his hind paws, put his front paws on the edge of the table and had a look. Oh! So that's where he was! He was sitting on the table, waiting for Vaska.

Then Vaska began doing such intricate leaps and twists from joy that the poor man felt the hair on the back of his neck rising. He forgot all about his pompous manner and bellowed like a drowning man:

"Help! Help!"

From time to time Vaska would stop his jumping to rise up and have a peep at the table. When the man would see his muzzle only inches away and his eyes burning with excitement he would wave his perfumed handkerchief and moan:

"Oh, dear! Somebody! Somebody help!"

We heard this moaning and came running into the dining room to see what had happened. We froze in the doorway: there, on our festive table, squatting right beside our lovely birthday cake, was Father's clerk, all pinched and green from fright. His glassy eyes stared at the floor in horror, as if a raging mammoth were rushing at him, when actually there was no one there but Vaska, whose whiskers were sticking straight up from laughter.

We all burst out laughing. The visitor kept a wary eye on Vaska and managed a crooked smile, but he did not have the courage to get off the table.

Then Father came in. He helped the man down, straightened his suit and apologised for Vaska's behaviour. He even poked Vaska with his toe and spoke to us in a very stern voice:

"Stop it! There's nothing to laugh about. Get this creature out of here!"

We took "this creature" by the front paws and walked him out of the house and into the garden, where we laughed till our sides nearly split.

All spring, summer and autumn we patted and spoiled Vaska, but when the leaves fell and the orchard became bare, we suddenly noticed that Vaska was quite a big tiger.

He was gradually giving up his childish games for more serious ones: tracking, stalking, wrestling and jumping.

He had had some of the traits of a grown tiger since infancy: he had always liked to creep up silently and pounce on various animals and birds. As he grew older these traits became more pronounced.

Vaska never touched another chicken after his unsuccessful encounter with the hen, and especially after he had been punished for snatching the rooster. But he had never forgotten the pleasant feel of feathers or the rooster's limp body in his mouth.

146

And so he made up a new game.

He would slip into the nursery to play when there was no one there.

His favourite game was to pull a pillow off the bed, chew open one of the corners and then smack the pillow with his paw, sending a cloud of feathers flying in all directions. And then he could sink his teeth into the pillow and growl.

Why, it was practically the same as hunting a wild bird!

We would come running at the sound of his snarling and growling and catch Vaska at the scene of the crime. There was the pillow on the floor, there was Vaska on top of it with a ferocious expression on his face and feathers all over him.

"What's the matter? Are you teething?" we'd grumble, snatching away our possessions. "Why, he can't seem to let anything alone! He has to get his teeth into everything!"

We soon thought of a way out. We gave Vaska a present of his very own, an old felt boot. We would drag the boot along on a string and Vaska would pounce on it like a cat tracking a mouse. After playing with him for a while, we let him have the boot. It served as a wonderful distraction, for as long as he had it in his mouth, he never touched anything else. He would set off proudly, carrying the felt boot.

Vaska loved to watch the horse. In the daytime, when it was let out to graze in a fenced-off part of the

orchard, he would hide in the bushes and spend hours
watching it.

Our favourite game was played as follows:

We would put our dolls in our little wagons and set
out through the lilac thicket to a small clearing where
the dolls lived.

Sonya, Yulia and Natasha pulled the wagons along
a narrow path. I rode beside them on a stick that was
my favourite steed, Whirley.

As we trudged along we'd say: "Wild beasts often
attack the villagers in these parts."

By then Vaska's huge eyes could be seen glittering
in the bushes. He followed the wagons like a cat,
ready to pounce at any moment.

By then we had nearly reached the clearing. The

most dangerous and overgrown path lay ahead. We came to a bend and the wagons disappeared behind the curve, first one, then the others.

Suddenly a tiger came bounding out to attack the caravan. The peaceful villagers shrieked and howled as he grabbed a doll and disappeared with it into a far corner of the orchard, which was now a make-believe jungle.

We would hastily reach for our guns (sticks with raw potatoes stuck on the ends) and set off to rescue the kidnapped "child". Often, when Vaska retreated under a hail of potato bullets and the battle was over, we'd find the poor "child" minus her wig and with the stuffing coming out.

Then we'd discover the wig and bonnet in Vaska's mouth.

Soon Vaska thought up a new game. He was jumping on trees.

There was an old branching tree opposite the house. We hung a piece of felt from one of the branches and watched Vaska jump for it. The felt was about two metres off the ground. Vaska would crouch, take aim and leap. Then he would sink his teeth and claws into the felt and every muscle in his lithe, feline body rippled as he swung from the branch.

When he had had his fill of swinging, he would jump down, circle the tree silently a few times and then take aim again. His eyes glittered like live coals, his whiskers stood up on end and his tail twitched.

When Vaska stretched out on the couch now, it was too small for him.

We continued our happy games, but our parents kept thinking a change would soon have to be made in Vaska's way of life.

One day an unpleasant and cowardly woman went to see the Mayor. She clucked and sighed and complained about Vaska, saying:

"Mercy me! How can such a thing be tolerated! Why, there's a tiger loose in the town! I feel faint just thinking of it! Who can tell what he'll do next? Why should we run such a risk? Why should we court trouble and danger?"

The Mayor summoned Father and told him that he would not be allowed to have Vaska roaming around and would have to put the animal in a cage. Meanwhile, until the cage was ready, the tiger would have to be chained.

We had no choice but to obey his order.

At first, Vaska could not get used to his chain. He would growl in an insulted voice: *achm!*

He looked so upset that though we had agreed not to let him loose, we would untie him when there were no grown-ups about (and the grown-ups would untie him when we were not about).

Then Vaska would race around the orchard as before, stretch out on the couch and leap up to catch his piece of felt on the tree. He was exercising his stiff muscles.

The days slipped by, but there was still no cage.

We did not have enough money to order a big, strong cage, and there was no sense ordering a small one, for we would never have kept Vaska cooped up in it anyway.

Father was waiting for new unpleasant developments from the Mayor's office and was upset and cross. As ill-luck would have it, a merchant happened by. "Sell me your tiger! Sell me your tiger! I'll feed him very well. I'll build him a huge and wonderful cage. He'll live like a king."

Both Mother and Father were very reluctant to do so, for neither of them wanted to say good-bye to Vaska. But it's very expensive to keep a tiger. Besides, all the neighbours were displeased, and were beginning to complain about Vaska. This and many other things made my parents hesitate. As if that were not enough, Vaska got into some more trouble.

Once, about noontime, Father heard a terrible scream. He rushed out to see what had happened. Mother was running down the porch steps. She was shouting and pointing towards the fence.

There, next to the fence, was a small wild goat. Perched on top of it, with his claws bared, was that wretch Vaska, his eyes bulging with joy.

At the sight of Father running towards him he jumped off the goat and ran away. Luckily, Vaska was still afraid of Father, ever since that memorable day when he had slammed him against the fence for catching the rooster. Still, he tried to claw Father's boot as he made his escape.

After this we were forbidden to let Vaska loose and he spent his days chained up. Ten days later Vaska was up to his old tricks again. This time he got loose all by himself and caught a colt. True, he didn't have a chance to hurt it, but he did snap at someone and bit him hard. This made my parents finally decide that Vaska had to go.

They summoned the merchant (who supplied animals to zoos) and made him promise that he would treat Vaska well and would never sell him to a zoo.

We could not believe that Vaska would soon be taken away and began to wail so loudly that our parents shooed us off to the orchard. The cunning merchant followed us there. He offered us sweets and invited us to come and see his own zoo, saying that he loved animals.

Besides, he asked us to tell him all about Vaska's ways and habits. At first we didn't even want to speak to him, but we finally gave in and showed him how we fed Vaska, how we bathed him and cared for him. Still, we watched him suspiciously and kept making him swear by all that was holy that he would love Vaska.

"But he probably doesn't need your love at all," we added rudely and went off to grieve.

The sad day finally dawned.

One autumn evening, when crows were cawing in the empty orchard, a squeaky wagon rolled into the yard. There was an iron cage on the wagon.

Father tried to joke about it with Mother but his hands trembled as he untied Vaska. Vaska pressed close to his legs in fright as they both walked up the plank and into the cage. But when Father went out, leaving Vaska alone inside, he screamed and kept throwing himself against the iron bars. Then, whining pitifully, he stuck his front paws through the bars towards Father. He and Mother stood there in silence, shaken by Vaska's despair.

News that Vaska was being taken away finally reached us. We left our toys and came running into the yard and stopped the wagon just as it was starting.

"Vaska! Dear, sweet Vaska!" we whispered in shaky voices, pressing our faces against the bars, while Vaska purred at us from inside the cage, saying *"Ooff, ooff!"*

There were tears in Mother's eyes. As soon as the wagon started up again we snatched our coats and ran after it. Thus, holding on to the bars of the cage, we walked alongside and saw Vaska to his new home. We stayed there till very late, helping to settle him in his huge new cage. We made him a soft bed of hay, patted him, and said in parting:

"Tomorrow we'll come back to see you at the crack of dawn."

We had to leave. There, in the cage, our tiger

howled pitifully, having been left all alone for the first time in his life.

Early the next morning we raced off to see Vaska. We woke the watchman who slept in the garden near the animals and demanded that he let us in.

"We didn't come to see your animals," we kept saying, for he did not want to let us in. "We just came to see Vaska. D'you understand? We've come to see our tiger. He's ours, we have a right to."

We pushed past him and ran down the path so quickly that he merely shrugged.

We thought that something terrible must have certainly happened to Vaska during the first night he had spent without us. We saw a cage at the far end of the path. A live and healthy tiger was gazing intently at us. He had heard us as we were arguing with the watchman and had jumped up to greet us.

Sonya was the first to reach him.

"How are you, Vaska dear?" she shouted.

Vaska crinkled his whiskers in a smile and answered "*Ooff, ooff!*" He offered us his paw through the bars and each one of us shook it in turn.

We washed the floor of his cage and dried it with rags. We shook out the straw and said that his bowl should have been washed better, because Vaska was squeamish and would not eat from a dirty bowl. We inspected everything he was given to eat very carefully. Later, we told our parents how Vaska was getting along, and on Father's first

154

day off he and Mother accompanied us on our visit.

Oh, how happy Vaska was! Father opened his cage and let him out to have some exercise in the huge garden. Vaska jumped, rolled around in the grass and kept rubbing against Father's legs, licking his hands, putting his paws around him and never letting him out of his sight. He seemed to be smiling under his whiskers and chortling all the while.

Then, after we had played and fed him, it was time to leave. Vaska followed Father trustingly into the cage. But suddenly Father darted out again and closed the door. Vaska was even ready to accept this. He continued to purr, even though he had been locked in, and he rubbed his head against the bars. But this only lasted until we began moving towards the exit and passed through the gate.

Then Vaska threw himself against the sides of the cage, and roared in despair. It was terrible to hear him.

Vaska's new owner tried to be as attentive to him as we had been but he did not really like animals and regarded them only as a profitable business. Besides, he was terribly afraid of Vaska.

Fortunately, a Kazakh named Ismail, who used to live with us and always loved and spoiled Vaska, agreed to go over to Vaska's new owner for the sole purpose of caring for the tiger. This made Vaska's life much happier. With Ismail there to look after him, Vaska was not as homesick as before. His life was not bad at all and he had as much to eat as he wanted.

In time we became used to the fact that Vaska lived several blocks away from us. When school started we could only come to visit him on Sundays. Each time we came we noticed how much he had grown during the week. In a month's time he had become a huge, powerful tiger.

One day Vaska's new owner came running to our house. He was so upset he could not even tell Father what was wrong, but in between his gasps and exclamations, Father realised that something had happened to Vaska. He grabbed his hat and hurried to his aid.

He saw that the cage door was open and the cage was empty. Ismail came up and said that Vaska was in the house. When Vaska's owner heard that, he ran off to fetch the veterinary, while Father went in to see Vaska.

He was stretched out to his full length on the floor, breathing heavily. His collar had been removed. Father bent over him, patted him and called him by name, but Vaska did not respond. It was too late to help him. Several minutes passed. Vaska sighed deeply and died.

Father was terribly upset. He asked Ismail what had happened.

"Did anyone beat him? Perhaps someone poisoned him?"

"Oh, no. It all started long ago. The last few days he seemed very sleepy and listless. He didn't want to run, he didn't want to play, but kept lying down. This morning, when I came into his cage, he didn't even raise his head. I tried to get him up and saw that he was breathing with great difficulty. Then I sent the master for you and managed to drag him into the house. I thought maybe he'd perk up a bit indoors. Poor Vaska!"

Father helped the veterinary surgeon with the autopsy and the diagnosis was that he had died from an adipose heart. Vaska had simply been too fat. He had been getting too much meat, and fat meat at that, and a lot of water, while at our house he had had soup, milk and eggs and much less meat. And he had had too little exercise here, too.

When Father came home he did not know how to break the sad news to us. We wept bitterly over the death of our darling tiger and promised each other that we would never forget him and would tell all the children about him.

FRANTIK

"Wait!" Sonya said, looking into the baby fox's sad, angry eyes. "Why don't you feed him, instead of annoying him with all your chatter?"

The little fox was sitting in a corner behind the bed. His shining eyes glittered as if they were filled with tears.

He was very tiny and seemed to be made of a fluffy little tail and a pair of tiny pointed ears.

Fedot Ivanovich, one of the foresters, had ridden up to the house several hours before and called to us. When we had all come running, he had untied the string of the sack he was holding and pulled out a little shivering bundle of fur.

At first we thought it was a grey kitten.

"Here, Sonya," Fedot Ivanovich had said. "Take him into the house and see that no one frightens him. He's frightened enough as it is."

Sonya carried the fox-cub into the room. The minute she put him down, he trotted into a far corner behind the bed and turned his back to the room.

Seeing how frightened he was, we sat down in a semicircle on the floor and spoke in whispers.

"How bea-u-tiful he is!" Natasha breathed, peeping behind the bed.

She wanted to pat him, but the moment she extended her hand, the cub arched his back threateningly, shifting his tiny feet, and gave forth a strange, jerky bark: *kakh, kakh, kakh!* He seemed to be coughing, while something in his throat was making a funny *nngrrrr* sound.

"What do foxes eat?" Natasha asked, pulling away her hand. "I guess they eat roosters, don't they?"

"We-e-ll, they probably do," Sonya answered gravely, "but we can't give him any of the chicks. You'd be the first to scream if we gave him your Clucky or Chickey. And then, he's still very small so he should have milk. Go bring some milk in a saucer."

Natasha hopped off on one ,foot, while Sonya picked up the fox and settled down on the floor again, cradling him in her arms.

"Nice little foxy, sweet little foxy," she cooed.

But the fox's fur bristled and he pushed away from her with all four paws.

Sonya pressed him down in her lap and scratched behind his ear gently. He seemed to like this and stopped squirming.

The little cub stared at Sonya, looking right into her eyes. Then, putting his trust in her, he pressed his furry head against her chest. By the time Natasha returned, he had no intention of running off into the corner again, but merely snuggled deeper under Sonya's arm.

Natasha set the saucer of milk on the floor, while Sonya pushed his nose towards the milk. He sniffed loudly, tumbled off her lap and pranced excitedly around the saucer, barking his funny *kakh, kakh, kakh! Ngrrr!*

Then he stood right over the saucer, arched his back and shielded it from us. He kept looking at us anxiously, as if he was afraid we'd lap up his milk.

"Let's move away," I said. "He's worried and he's not eating."

We all hid. Sonya alone remained beside him.

The little fox looked at her suspiciously again and then began to lap up the milk. His tongue was long and sharp, with a funny hook on the end. He drank as neatly as a cat and as quickly as a puppy. He had been very hungry and now there was such pleasure on his face and a smile under his whiskers. His eyes closed with delight, while his tiny black feet shivered with greed.

The fox-cub was the size of a small cat. His legs were rather strong, but his body was small, bony and light as a feather. His neck was really very skinny, but his fluffy fur made it look round and firm. He had a large head with a quivering black pointed nose, pointed ears and button eyes. His fur was greyish-yellow with dark feet and dark hair on the tips of his ears; his jowls, neck and stomach were white.

When he had finished the milk he pulled a piece of milk-soaked bread out of the saucer, licked it dry, picked it up in his teeth and ran over to the stove.

He put the bread on the floor and began sniffing at the little pile of sand which we kept near the stove for cleaning knives. He apparently didn't like the smell of the sand, for he picked up his piece of bread and began journeying round the room with it.

"What's he looking for?" We hung our heads over the sides of our various hiding places and followed his movements with interest. After exploring each and every corner, he finally returned to the stove. There he began digging a hole in the sand, never letting go of the crust. He put it in the hole, pressed it down with his nose and covered up his treasure carefully. Then, he turned around and did his duty right on the place where he had buried his food!

"Oh, no! You can't do that!" Sonya cried.

The cub jumped at the sound of her voice. He

turned towards her and began waving his tail and muttering. He was probably trying to explain that it was just what foxes usually did, just like people put food away in a cupboard.

"Well, all right," we said, though we didn't quite understand his explanation.

We heard Mother's steps and quickly cleaned up the mess before she came in.

By supper time the little fox had sniffed at and examined everything in the room and had had a good nap on his blanket in the corner. As he slept Natasha sat guarding him on the trunk near the door with a little stick in her hand.

The cub was on her lap at the table and she was fishing pieces of meat out of her soup plate and feeding them to him.

"Put him down this minute," Father said when he noticed what she was doing. "He won't starve. Eat your dinner properly!"

When we were having tea Mother gave the cub a lump of sugar, which made him very happy. He chewed it into many tiny pieces and then licked them up from the floor one by one, crunching them slowly with the greatest of pleasure.

"What shall we call him, Uncle Fedot?" we asked our favourite forester, as we crowded round him. "It's your present, so you name him."

"Well, that's a very serious problem," Fedot Ivanovich said. "You can't just give him any old name. He has to have an interesting name. You know, my friend had a little white dog with a very sharp muzzle and its name was Jip. Let's call our dandy Jip, too. What do you say?"

"Oh, no! Why Jip? What kind of a name is Jip?" Natasha said unhappily. "Let's call him Frant* instead. All right?"

"Frant. Frántik. Hm. It's not a bad name at all," we agreed.

Meanwhile, Frantik was busy exploring the room. Suddenly he made an interesting discovery: he found a basket of eggs under the bench near the stove. He rose up on his hind legs and peeped into the basket. My, how many eggs there were! He seemed puzzled, for what could a tiny fox do with such a great number of eggs? Finally, he decided that he would try his best anyway.

Without wasting another moment, he picked an egg out of the basket and carried it into the other room in his mouth. He jumped onto one of our low beds, scratched away the blanket, pushed the egg far under the pillow, pressed the pillow down and set off for another egg.

He had a harder time with the second egg and kept running around until he finally came upon a felt slipper. He sniffed at it and then pushed the egg into the toe. Then he set out for the third egg.

---

* *Frant* (Russ.)—dandy.

When Fedot Ivanovich noticed what he was doing he said:

"Well, Frantik, you certainly are a fast worker!" And he picked up the basket and set it on the bench.

Frantik had been caught red-handed. He tried to escape behind the trunk, but when Sonya looked behind it he realised he would not be able to hide the egg anyway. So he bit a hole in the shell, sucked the egg out and licked his chops.

True, he was quite full already, but after all, one did not abandon an egg, did one?

Frantik was no longer shy, his face was merry and very comical, his eyes glittered mischievously and his stomach was as round as rubber ball after his big dinner.

He curled up on Sonya's lap and watched the moths and beetles buzzing near the lighted lamp.

Before going to bed Mother settled Frantik down for the night in a little empty cupboard.

As she was turning down Natasha's bed, she found the egg Frantik had hidden under the pillow.

"Good for Natasha!" she said, laughing. "Look, she's laid an egg!"

Everyone laughed but Natasha. She said she hadn't laid the egg at all and finally burst into tears. We stopped teasing and said it was all Frantik's doing.

"See, Mamma," she said accusingly. "Frantik laid it and you said it was me."

This was so funny that we forgot to scold Frantik. Later that evening, however, when Father put on his slippers he became very angry, for he squashed the egg and got his foot and slipper all gooey. He said Frantik was a miserable creature.

At first, Frantik lived indoors with us. But since we were forever in the yard or in the orchard, he felt lonely and would timidly creep out on the porch.

He was quite used to people by now and was only bothered by the dogs and the little goat which often peered in through the open door.

One morning Frantik ventured out on the porch and curled up in a little ball in a sunny spot.

Suddenly there was a clatter of tiny hoofs on the porch steps and our pampered baby goat, Stepán, came up.

Frantik bolted towards the door in terror, but Stepan blocked his way. What was Frantik to do?

He lay flat on the floor, never once taking his eyes from the goat. Stepan stared back at him; then he snorted and rushed at him with his head lowered.

Though a six-week-old kid is not a dangerous enemy, he petrified Frantik. He waited for his chance and scampered past Stepan like a mouse — into the room and under the bed.

Stepan trotted in after Frantik and stuck his head under the bed.

Frantik felt quite at home in the darkness, it was just like his own den and not at all like being out in the open on the porch! He stuck his head out from under the bedspread fringe and barked in a very high voice: *Kakh, kakh, kakh! N-nnggrrr!*

Stepan became confused and backed away. As soon as he took his first step backward, Frantik gained courage and advanced, barking all the while. He raised his head and put back his ears. Now it was the bully Stepan who was in trouble.

We heard Frantik barking and came running to the rescue.

Stepan realised this was no goat business and jumped upon the window-sill, nodded mischievously to Sonya and leaped out into the garden.

Meanwhile, Frantik came running to greet us, wagging his tail happily.

"Poor dear! Look how frightened he is. See how fast his heart is beating!" We all patted Frantik and gave him a lump of sugar to make him feel better.

He couldn't bring himself to stick his nose out of the room for a long time afterwards and was content to watch us from the window.

As soon as we began playing ball, Frantik would take a seat on the window-sill and watch us intently. He was just like a cat with his fluffy tail curled around his front paws. He was becoming quite tame. He would eat anything we gave him: milk, bread, eggs, sugar, cooked vegetables, fruit, jam and even grass. But he had very strange tastes. For instance, after a lick of jam he would dig up a piece of old boiled tripe from among his stores and munch it happily.

He ate a little at a time but often and never discarded his leftovers, preferring to bury them, as he had his first crust of bread.

We were not very happy about this habit of his, for we would find bits of meat, bones and lumps of sugar in the unlikeliest places. Despite the fact that the windows were kept open day and night, there was a pungent smell of fox in the room where Frantik lived. Whenever the dogs wandered in they would sniff suspiciously. At the sight of them Frantik would come forward with his loud coughing bark and then flee to higher footing.

The dogs finally got used to him and stopped annoying him, but they never did become real friends.

Frantik, for one, never tried to make friends with any of the cats or dogs, and they simply ignored each other. He was always the loser in any of their rare encounters.

The hunting dogs could not understand why the "prey" did not flee and hide from them and kept getting underfoot instead.

"This is terrible!" Mother said angrily as she pulled a piece of mouldy cheese from my hat. "That fox will bring an army of mice upon us!"

"You're wrong, Mother," Sonya said. "He might

167

really bring in a few, but he catches them himself, anyway."

Since this was true, Mother had nothing to say.

Frantik loved to catch mice. He would wander about the room for hours on end, stopping every now and then to sniff at the cracks in the floor, pressing his nose to a crack, snorting in a very serious manner and twisting his head. Sometimes, as he was creeping about the room soundlessly, he would suddenly prick up his ears, stare fixedly at a spot on the floor and then pounce on it! That meant a mouse had run by under the boards.

Once Frantik caught a mouse. How happy and proud he was! He ran about with it in his teeth, playing with it like a cat. However, it all ended rather sadly for him. Right in the middle of the game, when he had left the half-dead mouse in the middle of the room and had run off to a side where he watched it with burning eyes, our cat suddenly jumped down from the top of the cupboard, snatched up the mouse and was gone.

Frantik raced about the room, but there was nothing he could do.

"See, Frantik," Natasha said, "why didn't you eat it right away? You wanted to torture it, didn't you? Well, it serves you right."

A month passed. Even though Frantik was catching all our mice and was very good-natured, he was causing too much trouble by living in the house, and we decided to move him to the yard. One morning Mother invited Frantik to go out to the yard, closing the door behind him. He ventured as far as the porch, but would not go down the steps and kept looking at the closed door expectantly.

"Come on, scaredy-cat!"

Sonya picked him up and set him on the ground.

He became frightened, ran under the porch and hid.

Unfortunately, one of the roosters had just noticed some grain scattered near the porch. He began scratching vigorously at the sand and crowing loudly to his hens. Frantik forgot all about his fright. He pounced upon the rooster, strangled it to death and ran off into a far corner of the yard, dragging the dead bird behind. Looking about stealthily, he dug a hole, stuffed his prey into it and scraped a little pile of dung over it.

Frantik imagined that he had concealed the rooster very well, but actually it protruded from under the thin layer of earth, with its legs sticking straight up in the air.

Natasha was sweeping the yard and soon came upon the rooster's feet. She pulled the unfortunate victim from its grave. It turned out to be her darling Clucky.

"I hate you!" Natasha cried as she laid the rooster at Frantik's feet. "You weren't even hungry, you choked Clucky to death for nothing!"

"He did it to spite you," Father said, and then added seriously: "I guess we'll have to chain the rascal."

We had always stood up for Frantik, but now we said nothing.

That very same day Frantik was chained.

Father stretched a heavy wire across the yard from the corner of the stable roof to the top of one of the porch pillars.

There was a pulley on the wire and a long thin chain was hooked on to it. The pulley rolled along the wire, leaving Frantik free to run back and forth across the yard. During the first few days he tried to keep off the ground, for he was afraid of the dogs.

The woodpile was near the stable and he made his home there. He slept curled up into a ball, he hid bits of food among the logs and would sit or lie on top of the pile, watching the people and animals busy in the yard below.

Frantik always liked to climb as high as he could. Often, when we were drinking tea or having dinner on the porch, we would call to him. Frantik would run to the porch, climb up the side and railing like an acrobat and get a tasty titbit for his efforts.

Once, Natasha went into the yard to share a candy with Frantik, but he was gone. What could have happened to him? Where could he be? Neither the chain nor the pulley were anywhere in sight.

"Frantik's gone! Hurry!"

We came running at the sound of her voice. It all seemed very strange. How could such a thing have happened? The wire had not been broken, yet the pulley and chain had disappeared. Father examined the whole length of the wire. When he reached the stable roof he saw the pulley and chain up in a corner.

"Here he is! I've found him!" Father shouted. "I don't see how he could have climbed up here, though."

The chain led to the hayloft.

A ladder was leaned against the stable wall at that point. Father climbed up and looked in at the hayloft door.

"Well, how do you do? Here he is, girls! Oh, you monkey!" Father said and laughed. "Come and see how grand he looks!"

Frantik had a killing look on his little face as he sat there pompously on a pile of hay, admiring the view through the door.

When he saw Father's head and shoulders appear, he smiled, wagged his tail and climbed on his shoulder. Father brought him down and said:

"Ladies, may I present a young nature lover?"

Frantik became shy and ran off to his woodpile.

There were five small plywood boxes lined up against the wall in the hayloft. These were the nests where the hens laid their eggs in summer. Every day at noon Natasha and I would climb up to collect the eggs.

Nearly all the hens were brood hens and we always found three or four eggs in each nest. Mother said that as soon as we had collected two hundred eggs she would give me a book and Natasha a doll.

We had collected over a hundred when we noticed that the hens were beginning to lay very poorly. We would find three, two and even one egg in each nest, and then, finally, none at all.

What had happened to the hens? Were they poorly fed? We tried giving them more to eat, but it didn't help. Perhaps they had become too fat? Sometimes hens will stop laying if they are too fat. We tried giving them less to eat, but that didn't help, either.

Natasha and I forgot about our games, our other animals and pets. We hovered over the hens, but we still had a very long way to go to reach two hundred eggs.

Early one morning we heard an excited clucking in the hayloft.

Natasha grabbed my hand and though we were quite a distance from the stable, she whispered:

"She's laid an egg! That's my speckled hen."

"No, it's not. That's the red hen. Can't you tell by her voice?"

"That's how I know. I can tell by her voice. That's the speckled hen."

"Let's go and see."

We climbed up to the hayloft and crept along, trying

not to scare the hens. Natasha moved her lips, whispering silently:

"She's in the nest."

"Is it the red hen?" I asked.

"I don't know, it's too dark to see."

She was inching along on her belly.

"I think it's the speckled hen.... No, it's the red...."

Suddenly, she jumped to her feet and screamed:

"Thief! Robber! Wait till I catch you!"

A chain jangled. Frantik jumped out of the nest and flashed by us.

So that's why there were no more eggs in the boxes! Dear Frantik was collecting them for us.

Could he have actually eaten them all? Perhaps he had hidden them? Taking no chances, we began searching for the eggs. Suddenly, I stumbled upon a little pile. There were thirteen eggs in all, concealed under an armful of hay. If we had not caught Frantik at his thieving, the eggs would certainly have been tossed down with the hay or broken.

Soon we found a second pile and then a third one in the corner. When we counted them up, we had twenty eggs. Not a bad store for one small fox-cub!

That very evening we put Frantik on trial. We decided to shorten his chain so that he could go no farther than the woodpile or the porch. But even then he managed to make havoc among our chickens, for he was a very cunning fox.

When we brought him his porridge he would shove

it around with his nose till it had all spilled on the ground. Then he would walk away, stretch out and close his eyes, playing dead.

The rooster would see the porridge, run over to the bowl and crow in amazement.

Frantik seemed sound asleep. You could even hear him snoring. The rooster would call to the hens. They would gather round busily to divide up the porridge.

Frantik would open one eye. *Bang!* In a flash one of the hens would be flapping in his teeth, while the others had scattered in terror.

Frantik knew that he had to hide the hen as quickly as possible. It took too long to bury it and, anyway, the dogs were sure to join him; that is why he would drag it up to the top of the woodpile and then drop it into his treasure house between the logs.

It was easy to drop a chicken down the hole, but he could not get it up again, since the hole was deep and narrow. This did not worry the robber at all: he was always well fed and caught the hens for sport, not for food.

The weather was very hot, and soon Frantik's stores began to poison the air.

"What's that smell?" Father said, covering his nose. "It's suffocating. You can't even cross the yard. I think Frantik's using something called 'Special Fragrance'."

One day Sonya climbed behind the woodpile and found the store of dead chickens.

This was really too much!

We hit Frantik with a switch after we had laid the dead chickens in a row in front of him.

"Shame on you!" Natasha stormed.

Frantik looked very offended as he climbed back on his woodpile. Then he turned around angrily and barked: *Kakh! Kakh! Nngrrr!*

Never before had we had such a quick-witted, bouncy animal as Frantik. He couldn't sit still for a

175

minute. If he was not asleep and not busy thinking up new mischief, he would be scampering back and forth from the porch to the hayloft or climbing the pile of bricks near the porch to reach the railing.

Frantik was absorbed in his stores, though they always got him in trouble.

The dogs soon became accustomed to Frantik's habit of storing away food, and while he was forever thinking up new and better ways of hiding his goodies, they were learning how to find them. In this respect they were much smarter than the fox.

For some reason or other Frantik felt that the only decent places for hiding food were behind the woodpile and in the dung heap behind the stable.

In order to keep the dogs away from his treasures he would drench his stores with his own pungent smell. But this bit of cunning did not help; on the contrary, it led the dogs straight to his hiding places. In time, they became so accustomed to his smell they no longer considered it disgusting.

Frantik was a happy-go-lucky fellow and since he always had as much as he could eat, he forgot about half of his hidden provisions the moment he had buried them. However, he did remember one or two very special hiding places and was terribly unhappy if, after a long and difficult struggle, he would finally manage to move a heavy piece of firewood with his nose only to discover that the bit of sausage was missing.

Then, angry and indignant, he would trot over to the porch with his tail between his legs, climb up on the railing and grumble *nngrrr* for a long while with his ears pressed close to his skull. In between he would cluck his tongue, as if to say: "They've stolen it. They've gone and taken advantage of poor me."

Frantik was never one for cleanliness. He would roll around in the dust and garbage and after a while bits of paper, shavings, and rags would get stuck in his fur.

"Look, Frantik's a Christmas tree again."

No matter how often Sonya tried to comb and brush the messy fox, she never really succeeded.

An hour after she had pulled out all the strings and rags from his fur he'd have managed to roll in the dust, visit the hayloft, get his tail full of burrs and play in the garbage heap, until he looked even worse than before.

Frantik always played alone or with Natasha. They chased each other, jumped about and played hide-and-seek. Frantik would run behind a log, lower his head and peep out. Though you could see the whole of him, he was quite sure that he was well concealed.

Frantik loved sweets. We were forever stealing sugar for him, despite Mother's warnings. We taught him to stand up on his hind paws and stick his nose into our pockets and pull out the treat himself. This would prove our innocence if Mother happened to ask where he had got the lump of sugar.

We would put sugar in our pockets and walk across the yard ever so slowly. Frantik caught on immediately. He would come running straight towards us, fish out the lump and dash off in the opposite direction.

"Didn't I tell you not to give Frantik any more sugar?" Mother would scold.

"We didn't give him any. He got it out of my pocket himself. I took the sugar for myself, and I'm sorry I don't have it now."

What was Mother to do? The sugar kept disappearing from the sugar-basin, yet no one could be blamed.

Frantik became so used to rummaging in our pockets that he would never let anyone pass without searching him first.

Once, as he was sitting on his woodpile feeling bored, the latch on the gate clattered and two people entered the yard: a woman in a light summer dress and a man in a raincoat with huge pockets.

Frantik stopped yawning the moment he saw them and climbed down in a business-like manner. His eyes were glued on those big pockets as he ran up to the visitors, jangling his chain.

"Oh, look!" the woman cried, falling back to the gate.

"Here, Rover! Here, boy! You won't bite us, will you?" the man said bravely.

No, "Rover" had no intention of biting anyone. All he wanted was a peep into the man's pockets. He just couldn't believe there was nothing tasty in those big pockets.

"Why is he looking at you like that? You know, I don't think that's a dog at all. Be careful, it's some kind of wild animal," the woman said.

In summer Frantik shed terribly. His matted fur hung in strips from his sides. His tail became as scraggy and skinny as a stick. And he looked wretched and miserable. When people saw such an ugly creature they couldn't quite decide whether it was dangerous or not.

Frantik solved the problem himself. The moment the man turned to speak to the woman, his little head was in one of the big pockets. Aha! Just as he thought. There was a piece of candy there. Frantik snatched it and made a dash for the porch. He sat down on the top step and began chewing it, muttering: *Kakh, kakh, kakh! Nnngrrrr!* The visitor realised that this strange creature had robbed him and he began to laugh.

"What a thief! I just couldn't understand what he wanted!"

"Did you see how he attacked you? I thought he would take a piece out of your side, but all he wanted was the candy! How cunning of him to have gone straight for your pocket!"

Father came hurrying out of the house and couldn't understand what had happened. The visitors were laughing, while Frantik was busy eating something and growling.

"It's one of the children's pranks," he said, realising what it was all about. "They taught him all sorts of tricks. I hope you're not offended. What a rascal! He goes poking into everyone's pockets."

Far from being offended, the visitors were amazed at the little fox.

As Father went on to tell them of Frantik's mischief, they were more and more impressed. Fifteen minutes later we felt we had known these wonderful people all our lives. They were two young teachers from the nearby boarding-school.

Mother offered them some tea. Sonya and I set up the samovar, while Yulia brought out the tea-things and chairs.

As the visitors drank their tea they kept praising Frantik.

"Isn't he lovely! How long have you had him? He's probably a lot of trouble. Would you give him to us for the school? He'll have a life of plenty there. We'll give you a pure-bred hunting puppy in exchange. What do you say?"

Father wavered, but he had not reckoned with Natasha, who was sitting on the steps and had heard the conversation.

"In the first place, Frantik belongs to me," she grumbled in her deep bass voice. "When I fell and my nose bled Mamma said Frantik would be mine. And I don't want to trade him for a scroungy old puppy."

The teachers smiled at her ruffled feelings.

"So you can go and choke on your old puppy!" Natasha added triumphantly.

"Natasha! Leave the porch immediately! Why, the girl is running wild here! You're no better than your Frantik."

Natasha marched down the steps proudly, picked Frantik up on the way and climbed to the hayloft with him. There, alone with him, she wiped away her stubborn tears as she told him how terribly they might have treated him. Frantik listened patiently but didn't seem the least bit hurt. At the very first opportunity, he stuck his nose into her pocket.

While Natasha was pouring her heart out to Frantik in the hayloft, their fate was being decided on the porch.

The young teachers were praising their forest boarding-school that had originally been set up for frail children who would regain their health in the pure mountain air among the pines. The school was not far from our house.

"You should have seen how they looked when they first came here! You'd never recognise them now. They're like a pack of hungry wolves, we can't ever feed them enough. They go climbing in the mountains, swimming in the river and are as brown as nuts."

"Just exactly where is this school of yours?"

"At the second bend in the road, near the foot of the mountain, where the bee-keeping courses used to be."

"Oh! Why, that's practically next door!"

"Yes, it is."

Mother and Father were thinking the same thought.

"It would be wonderful if...."

The teacher understood.

"If we could take on your girls? Is that what you meant? Well, why not? I think it could be arranged."

"Our two eldest girls go to school in town, but I would so like to have the little ones closer to home."

"I'm sure they'll like our school. The children have a lot of freedom. We've an orchard, a vegetable garden and lots of animals. One of the boys promised to bring his pet fox from home. Your girls could take Frantik along."

"I just know they'll be happy at your school!" Mother said.

"Natasha and I know how to take care of animals. We could feed them and keep them clean," Yulia said timidly, peeping out from behind Mother's shoulder. Both she and Natasha had been dreaming of going to school.

"Which one is Natasha?" the man asked. "Isn't she the one who suggested that I go and choke on my dog?"

"She made a mistake," Yulia said, coughing nervously. "She made a mistake, she got everything all mixed up."

While the grown-ups discussed the matter, Yulia tiptoed down the steps and into the yard. She called in a hoarse whisper:

"Natasha!"

"What?" came a glum voice from the hayloft.

Yulia climbed up and told her what had happened. Half an hour later the two girls approached the porch carrying the squirming fox.

Their parents were talking earnestly.

"Where are the teachers?" Yulia asked.

"They've gone back to their school. Well, Natasha, you really outdid yourself today! We nearly died of shame!"

The very next day Father hitched Gnedoi to the carriage, Yulia and Natasha put on their white sun-bonnets, Mother joined them and they set out. Natasha was silent and worried all the way. She was afraid the teacher would not want to accept her because she had been so rude to him the day before.

What if they only took Yulia, what would she do then? There were many children in the school, they would all study and play while she....

Natasha hunched over in her seat in despair.

The carriage rolled down the mountain as Gnedoi trotted along the soft, even road. They rode up another hill and soon the little white houses of the school appeared in the grove below.

"What a lovely place!" Mother said.

"Mamma," Natasha finally said, "I didn't want to say what I did yesterday. That's just how it came out. What I wanted to say was that their puppy is very small and it could choke, because we have so many bones lying around the yard."

Everyone laughed.

"All right, but don't try to think up any more excuses. The teacher is not the kind of man to be offended by a silly little girl. We'll forget what you've done, but next time think before you say something rude."

The carriage turned in at a new wooden fence that surrounded an orchard and two houses set back from the road. The sign on the gate said: "Forest School."

Mother and Father came through the gate and climbed the porch steps. They smiled as they looked back at Natasha, all burning with excitement, for the girls had remained in the carriage to await the verdict.

They did not have long to wait. There were voices in the yard. Then they saw Father walking towards the gate. The teacher was walking beside him.

Natasha blushed so deeply that tears came to her eyes. She turned away, thinking that the teacher would certainly remember everything and would get even with her for yesterday.

"Well! Hello, girls!" he said kindly and opened the gate wide. "Come right in. While your parents and I have a talk, you go and meet the other children. They'll show you around. How would you like that?"

The man's kind voice made Natasha feel shy and she started digging a hole in the sand with her bare toe.

"Kolya! Masha!" the teacher called. "Come here, I want you to meet Yulia and Natasha. Take them around and show them our pets."

Then he and Father went into the house again.

"What would you like to see first?" Kolya, who was only a bit older than Yulia, said: "The garden, the class-rooms or the animals?"

"The class-rooms first," the girls said eagerly.

"Come on."

Oh, what wonderful class-rooms those were! There were two large bright rooms with desks, blackboards and bookcases, and the walls were covered with pictures, charts and maps.

Natasha sighed so loudly that the cat that was sleeping on the window-sill woke up and dashed out of the room.

Then the children took them to see the kitchen. The pupils on duty were very busy. Some were singing.

It was just as exciting when they visited the garden.

Then they were shown the stable, the cow, the chickens and baby turkeys. All kinds of birds were singing and flying about in the large cages made of wire netting in the orchard. There was a happy family of tame rabbits in a large wooden cage with wire netting.

"Do you know who this cage is for?" one of the children asked Natasha. "We're going to get a baby fox soon and this cage is 'specially for her."

It was a wonderful spot. The kennel included a large clearing on the side of a hill which was also fenced off with wire netting. There were bushes and trees both inside and out, so that you could hardly see the fence.

"She'll be happy here," Yulia said. Then she thought: "What if Frantik lived here, too?"

Natasha had been thinking the same thing, because just then she said:

"I have a fox at home."

"Really? Is it tame?"

"He's very tame. You can come and visit us if you want to. We live up the road, in the canyon. You'll see, Frantik's very sweet. I know you'll like him."

The girls were feeling more sure of themselves now, for though the school children had a lovely school and garden, they didn't have a fox like Frantik.

"We also have a deer named Mishka, but he's a bully."

They wanted to show Kolya and Masha their pets, too.

"Come and see us whenever you like. You can play with Frantik as long as you want to."

"All right. Are you going to go to our school?"

"We don't know yet."

The girls floated home in a dream, for the teacher had said they could come as day students now, but as soon as the winter term began they would live at the school like all the other children.

And so began the daily trips to school, and the daily visits of their new friends to the house.

All the children liked Frantik. They spoiled him so

shamelessly that he decided he was really a very important creature and would not remain alone for a moment.

In September Sonya and I left for our boarding-school in town, while Yulia and Natasha, both beaming with joy, set off for school with a crowd of their new friends. They marched along to a song they had just learned:

Comrades, the bugles are sounding....

Their voices carried far in the clear air, while Frantik's chain jangled in time to their steps.

Mother stood on the porch, smiling sadly as she said:

"Look at Natasha! Even Frantik turned to have a last look at the house, but she's forgotten us already. Her thoughts are all at school, she didn't even look back to say good-bye to her own mother."

But Mother was wrong. Just before the children disappeared behind the bend in the road they all stopped, raised Frantik up in the air, waved their hats and shouted good-bye.

"Good-bye, children! Good-bye," Mother mumbled in confusion.

Now the house was empty.

After dinner Frantik would snore contentedly as he slept all curled up on a barrel. They had placed a large barrel on its side in the middle of a large enclosure. The barrel had neither a top nor a bottom, but two covered tunnels made of wide wooden troughs were attached to it from both sides. This was a fox's favourite type of "den", one that had two exits.

In rainy weather Frantik would stay inside his house, but today it was sunny and he was sleeping on the roof. This morning he had found a new friend. A fox named Liza had been put in his kennel. Liza was very sweet and lively and quite tame.

However, their first meeting had been rather chilly.

Frantik had run over to her, sniffed, and then forgotten all about her as he began poking in the children's pockets. At first, Liza seemed to have taken a dislike to Frantik, but then she began following him around like a shadow.

Now Frantik was sound asleep on the barrel, while Liza sat below, leaning her back against it. She was scratching her ear thoughtfully with her hind leg and would stop now and then to stand up on her hind legs and sniff at Frantik.

The children were very disappointed. They had thought the foxes would jump with joy at the sight of each other. They had been so wrong.

"Don't worry," the teacher said. "They're just trying to impress each other."

True enough, four days later Frantik and Liza were playing and jumping and rolling around as if they had spent all their lives together.

It was such fun to hide behind the trees and watch them play.

By winter the foxes had grown gorgeous new fur coats. They were healthy and lively and played very interesting games. The first snow fell at the beginning of November. Then the cold weather set in. The stoves were burning brightly in the houses and smoke rose from the chimneys above the white trees.

After New Year's, the teacher said:

"Let's build a wooden fence around the wire netting, because the trees are bare and they do not protect Frantik and Liza from the wind or from us, either."

"Why do they have to be protected from us?"

"Because if we leave them alone, they'll have baby foxes in the spring."

"Let's build the fence then!"

They set up a fence around three sides of the kennel and began waiting for the babies to arrive.

Sometimes at night they would hear Frantik's funny bark. After a while, he stopped paying attention to Liza. Soon Liza was getting fatter.

"Will she have babies?"

"Probably."

The children spoiled Liza, they kept treating her to all sorts of tasty things, always keeping a watchful eye on her.

"Now, Liza, don't fool us!"

In the evenings the teachers would tell the children about foxes. They said that mother foxes become very restless when they have babies.

No one should ever touch or even look at little foxes during the first few days of their life, because that makes the mother very nervous. She tries to hide her babies, she even buries them and sometimes she worries them to death.

"Now, children," the teacher warned, "I don't want anyone to go inside that fence until I say you can. The foxes' eyes will stay closed till they're about three weeks old. When they're a month old, they'll come out of their den themselves to play in the sunshine."

Soon it was March, then April. In the middle of April Liza had her babies.

"Please, don't go near them! Don't scare them!" Yulia and Natasha pleaded with the other children.

But the temptation was too great.

One day the youngest girl opened the trap-door in the side of the barrel "just to have a peep" and ruined everything. All night long Liza kept running back and forth, carrying her babies in her teeth. She shoved them under the roots of a tree and buried them in the cold, wet ground.

The next morning Yulia saw her dig up a tiny squealing baby fox and then bury it a second time in another place. Yulia ran to find her teacher.

"Hurry! Liza's burying her baby!"

He took the half-dead baby from the over-anxious mother. Her other three babies were already dead. They did everything to save the last one, while the children scolded Liza.

"Stupid fox! Murderer!"

"Liza's not to blame," the teacher said. "One of you either touched the babies or looked at them. Liza would never have tried to hide them otherwise."

As he said this he bent over the trembling, blind little fox he had wrapped in cotton wool.

"Will he get warm?"

"I don't know. He might. But if I give him back to Liza, she'll start hiding him again. I read that if you give a mother-cat a baby fox, she will nurse it. But where can we find a mother-cat?"

Without another word, Yulia and Natasha threw on their coats and ran down the hill to the nearest cottage. They had been sent on an errand there the day before, to take the old caretaker some newspapers. But, most important, they had admired his cat and her three tiny kittens. They pleaded with the old man.

"He'll just die otherwise," they nearly wailed.

"Well, you see, she's an old cat and she won't go to live any place else. She'll come back home anyway, and she'll bring her kittens back. They'll only freeze on the way. So the best thing to do would be to bring your fox here. She can nurse him till he's old enough to eat from a dish." And that is what they did. They brought the little fox to its new mother. The cat calmly accepted him as one of the family.

When Liza discovered she had no children left, she began running up and down the enclosure. She stopped eating and became very sad. At first, no one wanted to look at her for what she had done, but soon everyone felt sorry for her and began spoiling her more than ever. What happy temperaments animals have! Five days later Liza was playing just as merrily as before. It was as if nothing had ever happened. Meanwhile, the little fox was steadily gaining strength and feeling fine in his fox nursery school, as we called the cat's family.

The teachers never tried to discover who the guilty child was. They knew that this had been a terrible lesson and that no one would ever do such a thing again. One day the children were discussing what they would be when they grew up.

"I'm going to be a veterinary," a little girl said and suddenly burst into tears. "If I was a veterinary, I'd have saved the frozen foxes. It was me who looked at them."

The teachers exchanged glances.

"Now, now, Manya! You didn't know it would all end so sadly. Just wait, when you become a veterinary you'll help many other animals to make up for what happened to the foxes."

They tried to console her. To change the subject, they asked Natasha and Yulia:

"And what do you want to be, girls?"

"We want to learn how to look after the forests," the two girls answered as one. "As long as we have dense forests there will be a lot of animals in them. The forest is man's best friend, and the animals', too. That's what Papa says."

"That's a wonderful idea! When you grow up, you can be foresters and you'll be able to help your father. But never forget that all the animals have helpless little babies in the spring."

"We won't."

CHUBARY

We would never have seen hide or hair of Chubary if not for the accident on the mountain pass. He was a first-rate horse and no one would have dreamed of giving him to us children.

We first saw him in winter. All the grown-ups followed Father out to the stable, where they argued heatedly and measured him with a tape.

"What a beauty! He's too good to be true," they said when they returned to the warm room, rosy-cheeked and chilled to the bone.

We also went to have a look.

The tall, sleek stallion was prancing on the snow. He was tied to a post and was rubbing his head against it, chewing it, and stamping. His stomach was gurgling.

We came up closer. He pranced more nervously and rolled a dark eye towards us.

"Not a bad nag," Sonya said importantly. "But there's too much gurgling going on inside of him, and he jumps around so much you can't even pat him. Now, now!" she shouted in a deep voice and took a bold step towards the post.

The horse whinnied softly, grabbed Sonya by her hood and shook her from left to right.

"He'll kill her!" Natasha gasped.

Yulia and I began to shout and wave at Chubary. He looked surprised and let go of the hood. Sonya stumbled backwards.

"Crazy horse! He should be in a crazy house," she said bitterly. "Grabbing people by the head!" She was very pale.

In summer, when Father rode Chubary, people would run out to look at them. Dogs would crawl under the gate and try to cut Chubary off, but no matter how they strained their muscles, none had succeeded in even nipping Chubary's tail. They would all fall behind, yelping with rage.

None of the horses ever tried to compete with Chubary, either. It would simply have been a joke. What a grand sight it was to see him galloping the twelve kilometres from town to our house on the shore of Lake Issyk-Kul without ever changing his pace!

There was a lawn in front of the house. Chubary would round the lawn, stop at the porch and snort loudly as he arched his neck. After that he would breathe slowly and evenly. We would bring him out a chunk of bread or a lump of sugar. Chubary would pick the treat up gingerly with his lips and never once did he bite anyone's hand.

"Just look at him breathe!" Father would say proudly. "What a pair of lungs he must have!"

We'd stick our fingers under the stomach-strap and agree.

That is what Chubary was like. Then one day in the middle of the summer Father saddled him and took along provisions and they rode over the mountains to Verny, as Alma-Ata was then called, where Father was to attend a regional congress of foresters.

Nearly a month passed. Father was still gone. One night we were awakened by a thunderstorm. The wind and the rain pounded on the window. Thunder crashed overhead and lightning flashed in the room. I was just about to wonder if a person could be killed by lightning in his own bed, when there was a pause in the storm and we heard Father's voice in the other room. We were all excited and wrapped our blankets around our shoulders as we hurried out to see him. There were wet clothes on the floor. Father, wearing dry clothes, was sitting at the table by the samovar, trying to get warm by drinking hot tea.

"Oh, how red you are!" we said as soon as we had greeted him. "Are you sunburned?"

"I should say no!"

"You haven't forgotten your promise, have you? Did you bring us any sweets?"

"No."

"Why not?"

"Because I didn't, that's why!"

"Did you bring anything else instead?"

"No, I didn't bring anything else, either."

We exchanged glances.

"Why not? You promised...."

Father clapped his hands to his temples. His face looked pinched and he kept shivering as if he were freezing.

"Please, get them out of here," he said to Mother. "My head is splitting, and I have to waste my nerves on apologies and explanations."

"Father hasn't forgotten at all. He bought everything and he certainly would have brought it home, but there's been an accident. Run along now, don't annoy him. Be thankful that he's come back alive."

She rushed us out of the room and shut the door. We couldn't understand what had happened.

"What sort of accident could have happened to sweets in the mountains?"

"They probably got all wet and soggy and melted away in the rain," Natasha said.

"No, I don't think that's it."

"You've read so many books and you still don't know that people can get lost in the mountains."

Sonya jerked her shoulder contemptuously and felt for the heavy volume of *The World of Adventure* under her pillow.

"I bet if you were lost and had no dinner you'd eat anything," someone else muttered. "He probably ate the sweets himself when he was weak with hunger. Well, I'm glad he did."

And we all went back to sleep.

The morning after the storm dawned bright and clear.

The sun rose, lighting up the treetops, but the earth was still cold and damp. We went outside and headed for the stable.

"That's strange," Sonya said. "There's someone else here."

"And not a very pretty someone at that."

"Worse than our Chubary?"

"What a question!"

"But where's Chubary?"

We were all standing around a small, unsightly horse with fish-eyes.

The horse snorted, turned away and began munching the hay in the crib.

"It's not too bad."

"It's not paying attention to us at all."

"It's waving its tail."

"What strange eyes," Sonya said, and we couldn't understand whether this was a good sign or a bad one as far as the horse was concerned.

While we were discussing the new horse an old Kirghiz man came into the stable.

"Oho, girls! Hello!"

"Hello! Whose horse is this? Yours?"

"Mine. You like it?"

"Well, it's not bad, but that's not what we want to know. We want to know where our Chubary is."

"Chubary?" The man whistled, waved his hand and said: "He's dead. He's done for."

From early morning the garden gate kept swinging back and forth. The villagers knew that Father had returned during the night and were coming to hear the latest news.

Father was not feeling well, he had a terrible chill. He was lying in bed, covered with heavy sheepskin coats, and kept talking incessantly, telling them how he had made his way home through the terrible Koinarsky Pass.

We huddled in a corner, hanging on his every word, and yet, we couldn't discover the thing that was most important to us. What had happened to Chubary? No sooner would he get to the middle of the story than new visitors would arrive. They would ask him to begin at the beginning again, and Father would begin at the beginning. And each time he told it, he spoke louder and louder, he became more and more excited and confused.

"Hey! He is almost delirious," one of the neighbours cried. "Wrap him up warmly and give him some aspirin."

We were sent for the doctor, as the district hospital was not far away.

We ran all the way, found the doctor and gave him the message excitedly.

"It's very important!" we shouted, and hurried back home. We had to run, for we didn't want Father to finish the story without us.

"He said he'll be right over," we panted as we fell into the room.

"Sh-sh!"

Mother shook her finger at us.

Father tossed in his bed, he laughed, and then he began speaking very quickly:

"You should have seen him jump, how he jumped ... all's lost ... my gun, and the money, and the saddle. We have to get it, to help ... you should have seen him jump ... get help ... I'll be right...." He sat bolt upright in bed.

"Lie still now!"

The doctor came into the room.

"All's lost ... got to help..." Father said.

"He seems to be delirious, he has a very high fever," the doctor said.

Then everything became very quiet. We all walked around the house on tiptoe.

Father kept shouting about pulling someone out. He kept talking, and talking, and talking.

The next morning they wouldn't let us see him. Yulia listened at the key-hole and turned to us, saying with a smile: "He's talking like a baby."

She pressed her ear closer to the hole and stood there for a long while. We shook her impatiently.

"Is it very funny?"

Then she turned round and there were tears in her eyes.

"Go on and laugh," she said, as her face crinkled up sadly, "but they say he has an abscess in his throat."

Towards evening Father got worse. The doctor stayed with him all night.

Next morning another doctor came from the hospital. They talked for a while and then spread out some shiny pincers and scissors on the table.

Mother looked frightened. She was very pale as she followed the doctor into the room.

"I won't faint, I won't be in your way," she pleaded. "You'll see.... Let me help you, I'll be of help. Maybe I can hold something for you."

Then a basin was brought into the room. We were told to go outside and set up the samovar.

The doctors were going to operate. If they had not, Father might have choked to death.

Mother brought out some books and Natasha's toys.

"Don't worry, girls," she said, seeing how upset we were. "Just be very quiet and try to be good. I hope everything will turn out well."

She went back into the house, and we all tried to be on our best behaviour. If a handkerchief fell to the ground we all rushed to pick it up. If one of us pushed another accidentally we would immediately apologise and ask whether it hurt very much. Then Natasha said:

"Who pulled out Whirley's tail? And the saddle comes off. You did it, Olya! I know you did!"

"No, I didn't! You're always blaming me. You don't know who did it, but you blame me. Well, I've had enough of it!"

Sonya caught my hand just as I was about to pull Natasha's hair.

"Stop it! Don't you know you can't make a noise at a time like this?"

"She was poking around in my things! She spoiled my horse," Natasha persisted.

"All right, you old liar! You know what today is, you can lie about me as much as you want to. Go on, take advantage of my kindness. Why, I wouldn't even spit on you!"

"Good for you! That shows you who loves Father best."

I went off with my book and tried not to listen as Natasha hissed stubbornly:

"It's all her fault! I know it was her!"

Time dragged endlessly. The books and toys fell from our hands. We wandered back and forth idly, listening to every sound. Our dog Jika followed us about. She was as sad and upset as we were. She sensed that something was wrong and seemed to be asking what it was as she looked into our eyes.

"Go on! There's no time for you today," we grumbled at her.

Jika realised that she was to blame for something and decided to punish herself so that we might forgive her and be friends again. She went off into a corner of the porch, sat down behind the door and hung her head. Now and then we would hear her sigh, yawn nervously and whine.

Finally, the door to the sick-room opened.

The doctor and Mother came out looking haggard but happy and said that the operation was over and that everything would be all right. We jumped up, tumbled off the porch and raced happily around the house. Then Jika peeped out of her corner. She took one look at us and was a changed dog: she crouched, bounded into the air, threw back her head and raced ahead of us.

The forestry congress at Alma-Ata had lasted longer than had been expected.

Father decided to take a short cut home. He and a Kirghiz forester headed for the shortest but most dangerous road. They had to climb nearly as high as the pass to come down the other side of the mountains near Lake Issyk-Kul.

Towards evening they reached the snow-caps and spent the night with the shepherds. They set out before dawn.

Chubary had been in a stable in Alma-Ata for two whole weeks doing nothing. He had grown fat and stiff and he was feeling the strain of the journey. He got very tired the first day.

The narrow goat-path wound past moss-covered cliffs and over gravel slides. Sometimes, it went straight up to the top of a chasm. Then they would have to go back down again and seek another path; sometimes they would get lost in the middle of a rocky ledge, where Chubary would strain helplessly in every direction, with stones rolling out from under his hoofs.

The road was not for an animal of his size or weight.

Father saw his legs shake, his sides caved in and he hung his head sadly during their stops.

The other man's skinny little horse was more like a goat. It behaved quite differently. It was a local Kirghiz horse and was used to climbing the mountain paths. It would sit back on its haunches and slide down the steepest parts. And whenever the riders

stopped for a smoke it
would swish its tail calmly
and munch thistles.

The sun was at high
noon when the riders stopped near a steep stony cliff.
They had reached the edge of the Koinarsky Glacier.

The glacier valley was so white it hurt your eyes.
Only the black teeth of the cliffs, bared here and
there, were a warning that one had to be very careful
if one did not want to remain here forever.

The wind was sharp and ringing. Powdered snow
was swept along like smoke. The sky was becoming
overcast.

The riders urged their horses on. Chubary had
stumbled several times, he had fallen and skinned
both his knees. The Kirghiz forester's horse was

getting tired, too. The moment its master noticed the gathering clouds he began complaining and bewailing his fate.

Whooo! Whooo! went the wind through the narrow canyon. Suddenly, a great gust would change from a wail into a roar.

Chubary was exhausted. He could barely drag his feet. Finally, he came to a stop. Father dismounted and walked alongside. He tried to lead Chubary on, but the horse pulled back. Finally, Father had to drag him on by the reins.

It was no easy task to trudge along the steep, uneven path, dressed in a long sheepskin coat and pulling a horse. There, in front of him, was the Kirghiz riding his nag! And here was this healthy stallion, well-fed and strong, being dragged by its master. Father yanked at the reins in annoyance. Chubary threw back his head and backed away. Father lost his temper.

"Oh, so that's how it is! So you don't want to be towed, do you? All right." He mounted again and hit Chubary with his crop. He had never hit him before. Chubary shuddered and hurried down the ledges.

A huge cloud was rising from the canyon. It looked like a shaggy bear. The cloud caught up with the travellers, overtook them and blocked the glacier valley from sight. Now it became still darker.

A flash of lightning split the sky. There was a roll of thunder. One who has never heard thunder crack in the mountains cannot even imagine what it is like. It comes crashing down from the black sky, and the granite cliffs cry out in giant voices. Then the echo repeats the cry and magnifies the terrible chorus; it deafens and crushes you.

A person begins to feel like a tiny speck, lost amidst the raging elements, and even the bravest of men will falter when he realises how helpless he is.

The path was lost in the darkness and the riders advanced haphazardly. The storm had turned into a snow-storm. Now the darkness brought on by the clouds became the blackness of night.

The riders urged their horses on, they wanted to reach the edge of the glacier as quickly as possible. The forester assured Father they had no more than a kilometre to go.

Suddenly, Chubary stopped. Father shook the reins once, then a second time, but Chubary would not move. Father hit him with his crop. The horse was about to go on, but instead he shook his head stubbornly and side-stepped.

He seemed to sense that this was a very dangerous place, that there was no road. But Father urged him on.

Chubary reared up, took a tremendous leap and....

Father did not know what happened after that. He flew out of the saddle and crashed onto the ice.

A lot of snow had been blown in between the cliffs where Chubary had refused to pass. It had formed a bridge and was covered with a frozen crust. Though it might seem firm and strong, there was emptiness, someplace far, far below, where there was nothing but a great pocket of air.

When Chubary jumped he came down with his full weight on his front legs, breaking through the ice and sinking up to his chest in the snow. He made another effort and jumped again. Now his front legs were free, but his hind legs had sunk still deeper.

He began to kick frantically, and in doing so he dislodged a great mass of snow. Suddenly, the snow began to move. Chubary whinnied, as if saying good-bye to his master. And thus, standing on his hind legs, he began to sink slowly into the chasm.

The Kirghiz saw the avalanche. He could not see too well by the flashes of lightning and decided that both the rider and the horse had perished in the chasm.

He dismounted, sat down in the snow and wept.

Who knows how long he would have sorrowed by the edge of the cliff had he not suddenly noticed that his horse had gone off by itself. He crawled after it. The horse lowered its head, sniffed at the ground and picked its way cautiously. The man crawled along, rising up now and then to take a few shaky steps.

Finally, the snow ended. The horse stopped and looked back. The forester caught the reins and mounted. Two hours later he was sitting by a hot fire in one of the tents of the upper village, telling the men how the Evil One had carried the forester off into the chasm.

There had been a flash of lightning at the moment Chubary had disappeared. Then there was a long interval of complete blackness. Father rose and peered at the spot where his horse had just been.

"Oh, no! Oh, no," he moaned. "Chubary knew this was here! He was fighting to save both our lives."

He waited for the next flash with hope. He would see where Chubary was. If he could only get hold of the reins. Chubary would crawl out, he'd certainly crawl out.

A bolt of lightning flashed across the sky like a rocket and Father saw—blackness, and a white pillar of powdery snow that marked Chubary's grave.

Father was now alone in the storm.

He fell into a deep hole at his very first step.

He whistled and then shouted at the top of his voice, hoping the forester would hear him:

"O-ho-ho-ho!"

He stopped to listen. The wind was howling more fiercely than ever.

"It's no use! Even if he were close by, he'd never hear me!"

He felt chilled and pulled his fur hat lower over his ears. His fingers were stiff with cold and his greatest desire was to wrap the sheepskin coat tightly about him and lie down in the snow and go to sleep. But he fought this feeling and kept on walking, talking loudly to himself to keep awake. He tripped and fell and sank into snow-drifts. But he got up and stumbled onward, not knowing where he was going.

He kept tripping on his long sheepskin coat. Soon he was exhausted, out of breath and drenched with perspiration. When he reached some rocks he sat down to rest and smoke. But his tobacco and pipe were in the saddle-bag, and his horse....

"I must be delirious. Maybe it's all just a nightmare. Chubary saved my life. He can't be left there to die."

He shook his head in despair. Then he took a handful of snow, had several mouthfuls, and got up. His face was aflame, his head was light and his legs ached.

Finally, morning came. The sun was bright in the mountains, but the wind from the glacier was biting. Poppies bloomed bright orange against the blue sky.

Two Kirghiz riders got off their horses and bent over a man sleeping on a rock.

"Who is he?" "Where is he from?" "Where is his horse and his gun?" were the thoughts that passed through their minds. But, true to their tradition, they did not act surprised.

They crouched down and took out a little pack of chewing tobacco. Each man had a plug, and then looked at the other. It was undignified for a grown man to act impatient or to seem curious. So the men just sat there, chewing their tobacco in silence, spitting from time to time and thinking.

Soon a third rider came up. He was a tall, bony old man, and he had spent the night in the upper village. He had heard the Kirghiz forester's story.

"That's the forester!" he said. "So he managed to get out alive. The men from the village are getting ready to go searching for his body in the canyon. Come on, get up! You mustn't sleep in the sun!"

Father opened his eyes with difficulty. How his head ached! There was the sound of moaning in his ears. He looked at the three men with unseeing eyes and lay back again. Then the old man raised him up, put him on his own horse and brought him home to us.

Nearly a month passed. Father was well again. He kept whistling merry tunes all day long, eating heartily, sleeping a lot and laughing often.

We watched him grimly.

"Look at him laugh," we'd say when we gathered behind the stable. "Why did he kill Chubary? What did Chubary ever do to him?"

One day Mother told us to air our bedding. We piled up our pillows and blankets and set out for the yard like a camel caravan. The sun was blazing. Our pillows were soon as hot as if they had been in the oven. We turned them over and boasted to each other about who had done a better job.

"Mine's the hottest!" Natasha shouted. "Just try to sit on it and you'll jump right off!" She sat down, jumped off, and suggested that we all try it.

"I'm going to beat mine with a stick, so there won't be any germs in it."

We all began smacking our pillows with sticks.

"Now you won't get another speck of dust out of it."

"I bet I will." And I waved my stick.

Just as the stick hit the pillow, I heard Yulia scream:

"Oww! Look what you did!"

"Why did you creep up from behind?"

"Why did you wave your stick?"

"I didn't see you."

" 'Didn't see you'! You should have looked."

"What'll we do? Put your head back, or it'll bleed a lot."

At the sight of the blood Yulia began to cry.

Just then Sonya came running round the corner.

"Stop crying! Wait!" she said. "There's news of Chubary! A Cossack forester is on the porch, telling us all about him."

With this she disappeared, dragging Natasha off as well. Something about Chubary? News of Chubary? What sort of news could there be of him?

I shrugged.

Yulia wiped her eyes and her swollen nose with a corner of her pinafore. I felt very bad about what had happened and apologised. We made up and ran around to the porch.

The man was well into his story. His hat was pushed back on his head, his gun stood on the floor between his knees; he was speaking excitedly and waving his hands. Everyone was listening intently.

"Be quiet," we were told as we came running up. "He's telling us about Chubary."

"Well, anyway, I drank some vodka to give me courage, pulled off my coat and said to them: 'Well, you can go on worrying about your Evil One, but I spit on him. There's no such thing as an Evil One, anyway. Come on, tie the rope around my chest and under my arms and lower me down. And don't worry, I'll bring up the saddle and the bags.' They were happy, because their Kirghiz customs wouldn't let them go down. They tied ropes around me and lowered me into the gorge. I slid down the ice. It was as steep as anything! Well, I thought, if they let the rope go, that'll be the end of me! It's best not to look down, because you can't see the bottom anyway. Just a bottomless pit. There I was, dangling on the rope like a worm on a hook, when suddenly I came to a stop!· I was standing on a huge ledge of ice. I turned around, and what do you think! I thought I heard someone snort. Then I saw him. He was pressed against a wall of snow. He was all white and covered with frost!" The Cossack shook his head.

Then he continued excitedly:

"It was an animal, see, but how smart he was! He had been standing there all that time without moving.

Just rolling his eyes. I leaned against him and thought: what a fix! How could I help him? I yanked the rope three times. That was our signal. They began pulling me up."

Sonya turned away, Yulia pressed her pinafore to her face. Natasha came right up to the man and patted his knee with her sunburnt hand as she whispered:

"And then? And then what?"

"Well, the men crowded round me when I got back up. They said: 'Why didn't you take off the saddle and the bags?' I really got mad then. I said: 'Here you are talking about a saddle, when there's a live animal down there.' I said, 'We have to save that horse at any cost.' But they only shook their

214

heads and said: 'Oi, oi, how can you? You can't do that. If the horse fell down, let him die there. A man's life is more valuable than a horse's.' They kept at it, but so did I. Finally, one of the Kirghiz men said he'd go down with me. We took some boards and rugs and started down. We had a hard time finding him. If he hadn't whinnied, we would have gone right by, because he was just as white as snow."

The man stopped, pulled out his tobacco pouch and was about to roll himself a cigarette, but he never did, because we all crowded round with our impatient questions.

"Did you bring him up?"

"How did you manage it?"

"Is he really alive?"

"To tell you the truth, I didn't have much hope myself. But we managed. We pulled him out. We wrapped the felt rugs around him, then put some boards under his stomach and tied ropes around him. Then we began to pull. We pulled and pulled till we got him out. I undid the ropes. A cloud of steam went up from the big bundle. Chubary had warmed up and was beginning to sweat. His fur got all curly. There he was, all wet and so weak he couldn't even raise his head! I picked up the bottle of vodka, stuck it in his mouth and poured it all down his throat. He swallowed it and just shook his head. Then we covered him up with the felt rugs again and he just lay there, moaning. The Kirghiz men kept on saying that

215

he'd die, they kept saying: 'What's the use, he'll die anyway.' But I persevered: 'Give him time and he'll get his breath back.' Well, it turned out the way I said it would. He did recover."

The Cossack grinned. Natasha patted his knee again.

At first, Chubary couldn't even raise his head. He wouldn't touch food. But then, when he had dried off, he became as hungry as a wolf. The men gave him some oats, then they melted some snow in a pot over the fire and gave him some warm water to drink. Then they helped him to his feet. But he couldn't walk and kept falling. They took off the saddle-bags and saddle and, holding him up from all sides, began walking him slowly, down the mountain. Every ten or fifteen steps he'd fall. They would let him lie there for a while, then they'd raise him up again. The glacier was far behind. Soon they would come to the camp. But the Kirghiz men were exhausted. They decided to leave the horse by the roadside.

Once again Chubary's life hung by a thread. If he spent the night in the open he'd certainly fall prey to wolves.

Just then they saw a light through the trees, and a dog started barking.

Help was coming.

"He's alive!"

"Is he really alive?" the men shouted.

"Yes, yes! We pulled him out of his grave!"

In another hundred shaky steps Chubary reached the first tent and collapsed.

Shadows passed back and forth across the campfires. Scraggy pups came running up to sniff at the horse. Mares galloped by whinnying and snorting nervously.

But Chubary just lay there stretched out on the soft grass, moaning hoarsely and breathing with great difficulty.

Chubary stayed in the mountain camp for over a month. Soon we were getting regular news of his progress. Now Chubary could get up by himself, Chubary could walk by himself, Chubary had whinnied loudly for the first time!

We received each of these victories over illness with renewed joy.

"They're bringing Chubary home tomorrow," we were told at dinner one day.

"We'll have the stable all ready for him," Sonya said quickly.

Father glanced at her and smiled sadly.

Several days before he had been out on his rounds, inspecting the forests, and had stopped off to see Chubary.

"There's nothing left of him. He's my guilty conscience," Father said.

Natasha kept annoying everyone with her questions.

"What did Chubary have? Did something hurt him? Papa said he had some kind of conscience."

"A guilty conscience," Yulia said. "One of Chubary's lungs is no good. It got so frozen that it's no longer any use. He's supposed to have two good lungs, but he only has one."

"But what about his conscience?"

"Well, what about it? Why do you keep repeating what other people say? Sonya, is a guilty conscience a sickness?"

"Certainly. You can't imagine how sick people can get from it."

"And Chubary, too?"

"Who?"

"Chubary."

"My, what silly girls!" She turned towards me indignantly and said, meaning Natasha: "It all comes of little germs getting into big people's conversations."

We had always been so proud of Chubary.

Now, when we discovered he was on the way home, we decided to have a proper welcome ready.

"You know, our horse spent three days in an icy canyon," we boasted in the village, "and nothing happened to him! He just lost the use of one of his lungs. If you want to, you can come over and welcome him with us."

Next morning a whole crowd of village children joined us.

We started out with songs and laughter and on the way we told them about Chubary.

"When other horses just give up, he carries on! You'll see for yourselves!"

We walked on for about four kilometres. When we reached the end of the tree-shaded road we drank the water from our flasks (though, to tell the truth, no one felt like drinking) and turned back home.

There were many people on the road. There were groups of five to ten Kirghiz riders on horseback. There were other men on horseback. Huge wagons clattered on the stones. The riders had old nags and good riding horses, they rode oxen and even cows. We often saw Kirghiz men riding small skinny nags and their wives riding behind them on cows. The wife would be holding a baby in her arms, while the cow had her calf tied by a rope to her tail. The whole company would be trotting along in a lively manner, with the baby and the calf wailing at the top of their lungs, trying hard to outdo each other.

We stared at everyone on the road. There were people who were leading horses, or following behind them, but nowhere did we see our beautiful Chubary.

"They won't bring him today," we finally decided and set off for home.

"They won't bring him today!" we shouted as we opened the gate and entered the yard.

"Who? Chubary? Why, he's here already. You probably didn't notice him."

"What?!"

"He's here already?"

"How could we have missed him?"

"Where is he?"

In our excitement we could not slide back the heavy bolt. We pushed and shoved and got in each other's way.

"Here, let me do it!"

"No! You're not doing it right!"

"Wait, let me do it!"

We were all in a hurry to see Chubary, to pat him, to give him some sugar and feel him take the lumps from our hands with his soft, velvety lips.

He'd guess we were bringing him sugar and would whinny loudly and prance about with joy.

Finally, we got the door open. There, lying on the straw, was a bony, shaggy nag, as skinny as a skeleton. It turned its head to us with difficulty, groaned hoarsely instead of whinnying and began to cough.

"Is that Chubary?" we whispered in grief-stricken voices.

"Poor Chubary!"

"How could he have got like that?"

"So what! He's even better now than he was before! He's gentler. And see how smart he is!"

"He's so very, very gentle," Natasha said through her tears.

"Here, Chubary dear, here's something for you," Yulia said as she fussed about him.

Sonya and I were quiet for a long time. But when I finally opened my mouth my first words were:

"So that's what a guilty conscience meant. How could anyone give him away when he's so sick?"

"You're right," Sonya said with a sigh and added stubbornly, "we won't let anyone give him away!"

We sat around the sick horse till evening, patting him, talking in whispers, as if afraid we might tire him. We came to tea silently and there was a look of decision on our faces.

"Well?" the grown-ups asked.

"He's so good, so smart, so kind."

"But didn't you notice?..."

"What? He's much better than he ever was."

"Yes, he certainly is. I like him much better now."

"So do I!"

"Me, too!"

Our voices rang out in unison. No one faltered. Chubary needed our protection now. Well, he had no cause for worry. We would never let him down.

Mother looked at our excited faces.

"I think I have really grand girls," she said.

That evening Mother and Father had a terrible argument. They became so excited we could hear their voices all through the house.

"I won't give him away to anyone!" we could hear Mother's ringing voice coming from behind the closed door.

"But you don't understand! He'll die anyway!"

"So what! Let him! If he dies, then he'll die. But maybe he'll pull through. He saved your life, and now he's entitled to live out his days in peace and plenty."

"But I need a good horse for my rounds, not an old wreck!"

"That's fine! Get yourself another horse then. But let the girls have Chubary. If they pull him through, he'll be theirs."

At this, Sonya clapped her hands and cried:

"Good for Mother, good for her!"

She pushed against the door in her excitement and we all fell into the room.

The next morning we found Chubary just as we had left him the night before. The only noticeable change was the crushed and scattered straw. There were straws in his forelock and mane. He had been thrashing about, trying to get up. Yesterday's long journey had probably sapped the last of his strength.

When we came over to him he tried to rise again. He stretched out his forelegs and rose a bit with great difficulty.

But it was all in vain.

His hind legs and rump would not obey. Chubary fell over heavily, sighed and kicked. Then he jerked up again.

"He's getting up! Come on, let's help him!"

Sonya bent her shoulder to his side. I helped her.

We had once seen a carter do the same when his
horse had fallen.

"Come on! Come on!"

Yulia and Natasha were grabbing at Chubary's stiff
legs, trying to find a place to set them down.

"There he goes! He's getting up! Come on,
Chubary! Come on!"

"Oh!"

"What are you hollering about?"

"Well, if it'd been you...."

Chubary was now standing with his legs spread far
apart. Sonya's face was all twisted with pain: he had
placed one of his hoofs on her bare foot.

I rushed to her aid.

"No, not like that! Don't shove him. Just raise it up
a bit. There, that did it."

There was a huge bruise on her foot.

"That's all right, it'll heal," Sonya said.

Natasha found a scrap of paper in a far corner of the stable. She spat on it and stuck it on Sonya's foot.

"Otherwise flies will get on it," she explained in the voice of an experienced doctor.

Until Chubary was well enough to graze in the meadow behind the fence we brought him armfuls of grass. He lay quietly in the sun near the stable. The pile of grass near him never wilted, for we took great pains to keep the supply fresh. Besides, we brought him everything we could find that he might like: oats, chunks of bread, lumps of sugar. Whenever the cow's fodder was prepared, we'd never miss the chance to whisk off some bran or beets for Chubary. We would chop up dry clover, mix in some hot flour gruel, add salt to taste and feed it to our patient.

For a very long while Chubary remained bony and ugly, but in our eyes he was beautiful.

In the mornings we brushed him and combed him, braided his mane, forelock and tail, tying a bright bit of ribbon at the end of each braid. Natasha spent hours combing and braiding his mane and talking to him. Chubary listened to her voice and laughter with pleasure. He would lie on his side, his large head reaching to her stomach. Sometimes she bent over and whispered something in his ear. Then Chubary would shake his head. Natasha would burst out laughing and say:

"Really, it's true! Why are you shaking your head? Don't you believe me?"

Chubary was used to having us nearby, talking and fussing about him. He'd become very lonely if we were gone for long, and would whinny with difficulty in a rasping voice that changed into a cough. We ourselves were happier when we were with him. We would even come out to read near him.

"You might as well take your bedding out and live in the stable while you're at it," our parents said.

Our efforts were not in vain.

With each passing day Chubary was getting better and better. At first, he would wander about the yard, stepping gingerly. Then he began going down to the lake. He would stand there on the bank, dozing in the bright warm sun.

There was always a lot of merriment near the bathing docks. We would join a dozen village children there and spend the day splashing about in the water. When we climbed out Chubary would open his eyes and stretch his head towards us with trembling nostrils.

"Chubary! Chubary!" we called from the water.

He would raise his head and gaze intently at the blue water. When he recognised our heads he would pace up and down, neighing gently. Sometimes he even ventured into the lake. Then we would grab hold of his mane and pull him in. Chubary would balk. At first, he did not dare go in deep, but gradually he became bolder and finally took a liking to bathing.

Once Mother wanted to send us on an errand. She called to us in the yard. When no one answered, she went down to the lake. She stood on the little pier, squinting in the sun and wind, and called us.

In reply, a couple of dogs came swimming out, then Chubary's shaggy head appeared, together with half a dozen shouting devils.

Chubary was lost in the crowd of children that pressed against him. He came out of the water, snorted and shook himself like a dog.

"Do you know, he's really much better!" Mother said in surprise.

That was the last day of Chubary's illness.

Several weeks passed.

Then one day a happy shout went up from the yard. A sleek and gleaming horse galloped by the window. Astride him were four girls in red hats.

Sonya sat in front, holding the reins. Sitting behind with her arms around Sonya's stomach was Yulia; I came next with Natasha practically on top of the horse's tail.

Chubary was decked out like a Maypole with his mane and tail full of bright ribbons and a bunch of red poppies in his forelock. The show was very impressive.

"*Whoa-a!*" Sonya said, pulling at the reins. "We're going to town. Do you want us to buy anything?"

"Just look at them! It's too far to town, girls. You

can ride around here, near the house. And please be careful! See that Natasha doesn't...."

"Giddy-up, Chubary! Use your feet, boy!"

With the four red hats bobbing, Chubary cantered down the dusty road.

Now we spent half our days on horseback.

We rode with a saddle and bareback, we jumped over ditches and fences, we learned to mount and dismount. Sonya and I were the eldest and had no difficulty doing all this, but little Yulia and Natasha found that they were too short. Natasha had to climb into the saddle in three stages. First, she would pull herself up by the stirrup strap, then she'd grab hold of the pommel and slide into the saddle, and, finally, she would throw her leg over the side and sit up. But these minor problems never bothered her.

"Learning to ride isn't hard, but when you learn how to fall I'll say you're good riders," Father said.

All the next day we practised falling. The idea was to gallop by a pile of hay spread out near the haystack and fall into it. Actually, it was a very difficult thing to do. Our hands would pull at the reins of their own accord, and it was no fun to fall.

"It's very hard to fall nicely," we confessed to Father.

"Why, have you tried?"

"Yes. We couldn't do it. Sonya was the only one who could."

And we told him about our "exercises".

Winter was suddenly upon us. Now we could harness Chubary to the sleigh and he could take us into town to school each morning. He got so used to riding up to the porch at seven o'clock in the morning that as soon as he was harnessed he would come out, push open the gate, enter the yard and stop by the porch.

Sonya and I (Yulia and Natasha did not go to school yet) would come running out, tumble into the sleigh and shout: "Hurry, Chubary dear! We're late!"

Since everyone was usually busy at this time, Yulia would be our driver. She would climb on to the driver's box in her heavy coat, fur hat and huge mittens. Meanwhile, the daily battle was being waged on the porch between Mother and Natasha.

"I want to go with them! Why can't I go?"

"There's no need for you to go."

"There's no need for me to stay home!"

"You'll freeze your nose."

"So what?"

"You'll look awful without a nose. No, I won't let you go. Go ahead, Yulia!"

"No! Wait! Wait for me! Wait for me! Wait! *Aa-a-a!*" There would be a loud wail, then a shriek, and a moment later Natasha, beaming with joy, the tears still running down her cheeks, would jump into the sleigh and blow her nose loudly in triumph.

Yulia would whistle like a real bandit. Chubary would start off at a quick trot and we'd fly along the hard-packed snow.

Yulia was an excellent driver. It was something to hear her cluck her tongue, shout, and reassure the horse on the dangerous curves with a deep *O-ho-ho!*

On market days the road was very lively: there were one-horse, two-horse, and even three-horse sleighs, all hurrying to market.

Usually, however, the road was empty, save for two or three neighbours' sleighs. We'd usually challenge one of them to a race, coming up from behind, shouting:

"Let's see what you're worth!"

The air would be full of laughter and shouting.

Chubary would tremble from excitement as he pulled at the reins.

"*O-ho-ho*," Yulia would coo in a deep bass voice, while devils danced in her eyes.

The neighbour's horses would gallop on ahead, but we'd be very close behind. The road was narrow. Then, on ahead, opportunity beckoned.

"*Whe-e-e!*" Yulia would shout.

At this, we'd all jump to our feet. It was the most exciting moment, for it seemed as if someone had picked up our sleigh and put it down in front of the others. Now we'd be abreast of them: the snorting heads of the other horses would slowly draw behind.

Meanwhile, Chubary, becoming ever more excited, would increase his pace. Our delight knew no bounds.

"Take it easy! Slow down!" people along the road shouted.

"Easy now, Chubary! Let's wait for those turtles!"
We'd stop and wait for them. Their driver was a small, angry old man.

"Just you wait, you rascals! I'll tell your father what you're up to, and he'll never let you out alone again. What sort of business is it to let children out without a driver!"

"Why, what's wrong? Are we in your way?"

"D'you want to kill someone? Don't you know you shouldn't ride like that? I'm going to speak to your father today. I'll tell him exactly what's going on!"

That would dampen our spirits.

"You have an excellent lead horse," Sonya would say brightly.

"Now don't try to pull the wool over my eyes."

"We've never hit anyone yet. But you did. You bumped into someone yesterday."

"You watch your words!" the old man grumbled, becoming angry again. "One thing's sure, and that's that you won't be riding around like this any more."

What if the old buzzard really told Father? He'd say we were racing like mad, never even looking to see where we were going.

During our Geography lesson that day the teacher called on me.

"Since you're half asleep anyway, you might as well come up to the blackboard and show the class how one would travel up the Volga from the river's mouth to its source. Is that clear?"

I walked up to the blackboard. As I stood near the map, I kept thinking about the morning ride. "What's the matter?" the teacher asked. "Don't you know how to begin?"

And then I replied, as in a dream: "Certainly, I do. You have to be very careful. We're always careful and we've never hit anyone yet."

I had a hard time living that down.

People who had never seen Chubary before would not have believed he had spent three days in an icy canyon.

His former beauty and sheen had returned. The only difference was that he did not hold his head as proudly as before, his legs would sometimes swell up and, if the road was steep, he would be short of breath. But Chubary was nearly as fast on the even roads of the valleys as before.

One day we were coming home from school at a fast clip. Near the village we saw a man on the road ahead. Yulia whistled as we flew by him and we suddenly noticed that he was waving and laughing.

"Wait! It's Papa!"

"*Whoa!* Get in, Papa, we'll drive you!"

Chubary was prancing impatiently. Father came up and looked the horse over with the same broad smile on his face.

"Well! I see that my Chubary is his old self again. I guess I'll have to get you a donkey now."

"Oh, that'll be grand!"

Father was admiring the horse. He stretched his hand out to pat his neck.

But Chubary snorted and shied away. His ears turned back, his teeth were bared. There was a mean look in his eye.

"What's the matter, boy? Are you still angry with me?"

We could not understand why Chubary was acting like this. Father tried to pat him again, but Chubary bared his teeth once more.

"All right. That's all right. You go on, girls."

"What about you?"

"I have to drop in here on business."

Yulia waited until Father had a good start. Then she smacked the reins and Chubary flew by Father in all his glory.

We were both surprised and pleased by Father's promise. Now we'd have Chubary and a donkey, besides. We spent the whole day discussing the seating arrangements and finally decided that one of us would ride the donkey, while the other three rode Chubary. It was an excellent arrangement.

That day at dinner Father said to Mother:

"I see Chubary's fine again. I think I'll start riding him. I've promised the girls a donkey instead of the horse."

"Instead of Chubary?!" we gasped.

"Oh no, you don't!"

"First you let us have him, and now you want him back."

"Nice parents never do things like that," Sonya said and her voice trembled. "I know you'll tell us to leave the room, Papa, but we'll leave without your telling us. It's not nice of you at all!"

She rose and headed proudly towards the door. Yulia and I followed her in silence.

"Mamma!" Natasha said as she climbed off her chair and trotted after us. "Why don't you say something?"

Mother took our side. She spoke to Father in a low insistent voice.

"Well, I can't give away a strong, healthy horse, as if it were a toy," Father answered loudly.

"Why, he's no toy. He takes them to school and on all my errands. He does his job at home. He's no good for going on rounds with you now, because he might catch cold again. You have a horse for your rounds. And if that's not enough, you can buy another horse. After all, the girls nursed Chubary back to life."

"But the horse I want is Chubary. I don't believe in giving in to a child's every whim."

They fell silent. We exchanged worried glances. This is what had come of our showing off! What would happen now?

Chubary ended the argument himself.

He could never forget the terrible days he had spent in the canyon and the long illness that had followed.

He was mortally afraid of Father, of his face and his voice.

He would not eat anything from Father's hand and always put his ears back when Father patted him.

This displeased Father, for Chubary had always been very devoted. He tried to make friends with him again.

One evening Father was coming home in a very good mood. As he passed the stable he decided to go in and give Chubary an apple. It was dark inside. Father walked into the stall. The horse snorted angrily.

"Easy, boy! Didn't you recognise me?" Father said gently.

No doubt about it, Chubary had recognised him. He tensed and then suddenly kicked out at the wall with all his might.

Father made a dash for the corner. The horse was quiet now as it peered into the darkness.

"Chubary! What's the matter with you? Hm? It's me! Would you kick your master?"

Several days later a hot-blooded grey pacer was led into the yard.

"There's a saddle-horse for you!" Father said proudly. "It's just like sitting in an easy chair, with the wind whistling in your ears."

We gathered behind the stable and broke into a wild dance of joy.

Soon after that Father and Chubary made up, but he never tried to take our true friend from us again.

A new doctor had come to the Lake Village. He was a jolly fat man and his pockets were always full of sweets, fish-hooks, whistles and other wonderful, useful things. He called Chubary "Ice Age".

We liked the way he spoke and the way he used beautiful and scientific words. We were also quite fond of his pockets. The doctor's children were of our own age. And all would have been well if it had not been for the horses. The doctor's bays gave us no peace. Each day they galloped to school ahead of Chubary. However grudgingly, we had to admit that they were an excellent pair of horses.

From the very first day the doctor's children began teasing Chubary:

"What is your old 'Ice Age' against our Orlik and Zmeika!"

"Well, if Chubary felt like it...."

"Why doesn't he?"

"D'you think we race with any old...."

" 'Any old'! You're stuck-up, that's what you are!"

We stood it as long as we could. We'd been forbidden to race to school under threat of having Chubary taken away. But the doctor's children thought we were afraid and kept on teasing us.

Finally, we could take it no more.

"All right. Let's start out earlier tomorrow morning and we'll see who's best."

The very next morning we started out at six o'clock and waited for them by the road.

Yulia tied the strings of her hat tightly under her chin.

We looked back at the doctor's house.

The gate was wide open. The bays stood near the porch. Then all came out of the house, got into the sleigh and were off.

The horses' hoofs clattered over the bridge. Then they disappeared beyond the bend. Here they were now....

"Let 'im go!" I shouted in a voice that was not my own.

The sleigh began to move. My teeth banged together from the jolt.

We rode out to the field.

The race was to begin beyond the first bend and finish at the bottom of the hill, near the stone pillars.

We were too excited to talk. The frost was bitter, but Yulia pulled off her mittens.

"It's hot," she said, throwing them on the floor of the sleigh.

The horses were abreast of each other and galloping.

I shall never forget that morning. There was a cold haze above the white field. The sun was just beginning to rise. The two sleighs flew along the smooth, deserted road.

Yulia did not dare give our opponents a head-start (as she sometimes did), but tried to keep abreast of them.

Chubary was in magnificent form. We were waiting for the first broad ravine. All would be clear after that. There, beyond the bend, the road was so narrow that two sleighs could never pass abreast. If we didn't get ahead of them now, they'd finish first.

Yulia realised this and was doing her best.

We were close to the ravine now but were still abreast of them.

Beyond the bend was a hill and a small rise, alongside of which ran an old deserted road. It was shorter, but much steeper.

Yulia turned around and looked at us.

"Take the old road!" Sonya shouted.

And at the very moment the doctor's sleigh surged ahead, we turned sharply, flew through a snow-drift to the old road, soared down and then up and came flying out right under their noses.

"Oi, oi!" the Kirghiz driver shouted. "Good for you!"

Now we had to keep them from getting ahead at the narrow bend by the river.

We would hear the crack of his whip behind us. Chubary was flying on ahead along the edge of the bank. The stone pillars came into view.

This was the last bend.

Whoosh!

The sleigh tipped sharply and we all tumbled out on to the ice.

237

As I fell, I saw the bays flash
by and come to a stop at the
finishing line.

The sleigh had rocked back
on its runners. Yulia, though
badly bruised, was still on the driver's box. She rode
out on the road, stopped Chubary and watched
unhappily as we collected our hats and books. We
were all lame and rubbing our sides.

The doctor's eldest daughter and the driver came
running up.

"Are you all right? No broken bones?" they shouted
with concern, hardly able to conceal the triumph in
their voices.

"No, no broken bones," Sonya muttered.

They returned to their sleigh beaming, shouting something to us and started off easily again.

"Then we began to count our wounds..." as the famous poem goes.

Sonya had sprained her thumb, Yulia had cracked her lip, when she had hit her mouth against the edge of the sleigh, and it was bleeding. Natasha had a big bump on her forehead and a bruise on her nose and my whole leg ached.

We were all hurt. But who cared about that! The worst of it was that the bays had won the race!

By spring Chubary was really his old self again, the same old bully and fighter. As soon as someone left the gate open by mistake he'd be out in the street, fighting with other people's horses.

He would even manage to start a fight when he was in harness. If he saw a horse on the other side of the street he would prick up his ears, arch his neck and slowly turn the sleigh around. Then he'd come up to the horse and sniff at it.

They would stand there nose to nose, for a long time, arching their necks, stamping their feet impatiently. Then suddenly they'd neigh loudly, shake their heads and begin sniffing each other again.

This would happen if they were harnessed. If they weren't, they'd sniff each other for a second and then bite each other on the neck! Or they'd turn around and buck.

There were many horses grazing on the hills beyond the village in springtime. Chubary always tried to join them. If he did, he'd come home full of bites and bruises.

Once he received such a blow on his eye that a cataract began to form. We cured him by patiently blowing powdered sugar into his sore eye.

Another time he had a huge wound under his shoulder. We put liniment on it and chased away the flies that swarmed on the open wound. For a whole week we smelt like a hospital.

"Chubary'll run away to the horses and they'll kill him! Lock the gate! Chubary'll run away! Who left the gate open? Lock the stable, Chubary..." was all you would hear from morning to night.

We had many pets both wild and tame, but none of them demanded as much care and attention as Chubary.

Chubary's bad habits were also the cause of Natasha's argument with her kindergarten teacher. The teacher asked Natasha to tell her the difference between domestic and wild animals.

"The ones that live at home are domestic animals, and the ones that run away are wild."

"Well, name me a wild animal."

"A horse," Natasha answered readily, and then went on to explain: "Chubary is forever running away."

"Well, then, name me some domestic animals."

"A fox and a wolf. They don't run away. They just get into the cellar and the hen-house."

The teacher could only laugh at such an answer.

"Poor child! You're completely confused."

Natasha was very offended.

"I'm not confused at all. A stallion is the most runningawayest animal. But our fox only goes rummaging in the cupboard for sugar. I should know, we've had our fox for three whole years. And wolves, too. And nobody ever ran away."

They simply did not understand each other.

Then Sonya and I got mumps. Our necks were swollen and we were not allowed to go outside.

We were locked up in our room, isolated from the rest of the family, with a sign on the door which said "The Mumpery!"

It was spring, the sun was shining, the swallows had come back and the lilac was in bloom. All our friends were going to the big meadow for the May Day celebration.

Yulia and Natasha joined them. They came running up to our window, rosy-cheeked and sunburned, pressed their peeling noses to the glass, laughing as they spoke. Then they brought Chubary up to the window. He gazed in wonder at the strange shape of our faces through the glass.

There were wagons full of children passing down the road. There was the teacher from Mikhailovka with a flute, the teacher from the children's group with a guitar and someone had a camera. The crowd was growing steadily.

Spring was in the air, there was much excitement and laughter. Natasha climbed into one of the wagons, while Yulia and two of the doctor's children rode on horseback. Mother went out on the road to wave to them and to shake her finger at Yulia, "just in case". Then she came to our sickroom to give us our medicine.

"Why did you shake your finger at Yulia?"

"So that she'd remember to ride carefully."

Yulia was riding beside the wagon and all of Mother's words of warning were clear in her mind. But the doctor's children—oh, they were devils!—kept daring her to race.

What could she do but agree?

They let the wagons roll on ahead. Then they stood around in a circle and discussed where the race would be.

It had rained the night before. The damp field stretched as far as the mountains and seemed to disappear in the blackness of the canyon. There was a dead tree barely visible where the road disappeared.

"We'll go as far as the tree."

They counted to three and were off.

"Look, they're having a race!" the children in the wagons shouted.

Three heifers were standing by the roadside. They turned to look at the horses, waiting expectantly. Then their tails shot up, they mooed and bolted.

As ill-luck would have it, one of the cows fell behind and passed right under Chubary's nose. He tripped at full gallop and fell to his knees.

Yulia flew out of the saddle.

As Natasha told the story later, "I looked, and there she was, lying on the ground, and her head rolled away like a water-melon. I was so frightened! I jumped off the wagon and ran up to her and saw that it was just her hat. Yulia was lying with the eyes closed. Chubary was standing next to her, shaking himself. Then he began to shove her with his nose. Then some people came running and shooed him away. I shouted: 'Catch Chubary!' And then I ran after him."

The teachers had scarcely come to their senses when Natasha went scampering off after the horse.

The teacher from Mikhailovka raced after Natasha. It was a wonderful scene: a stallion was trotting and prancing down the road and following him was a plump little girl with her coat unbuttoned and her hat pushed back on her head. Galloping along at some distance, holding on to his glasses with one hand, was the teacher.

"Natasha! Natasha, wait!"

He waved to her and his glasses fell off. That was the last straw. The teacher squinted, blinked his eyes helplessly, then got down on all fours and gazed intently at the mud.

Meanwhile, Natasha was bravely carrying on, splashing along in her little galoshes, trying to keep Chubary in sight.

"Chubary! Sweetie-pie! Stop for a moment, won't you?"

Chubary seemed to have heard her. He slowed down and finally came to a stop. He raised his head and gazed at the cows.

This was Natasha's chance! She got rid of her galoshes, for they were in her way. One, two! Off they flew in different directions.

Natasha was closing in.

Oh, how hot it was! In no time, her coat and hat went sailing through the air after the galoshes.

"Chubary! Dearie! Here, boy!"

She gathered up the hem of her dress and raised it to make a little sack, as if she were carrying oats in it. The horse cocked an eye at her distrustfully. He shook his head, ran off to one side, and stopped to look at her again.

"*Whoa! Whoa!*" Natasha called desperately. She pretended she was mixing the oats she was carrying in her dress, as she came closer and closer.

Chubary stretched his neck towards her, his nostrils trembled as he looked into her dress.

At that moment Natasha grabbed the reins. She had him now! There was no need to pretend any longer, so

she dropped her skirt. Chubary did not want to believe he had been fooled and began searching for the oats. He snorted in Natasha's face, got the edge of her dress in his teeth and yanked at it. He even nipped her in the stomach and butted her until she finally slapped his large shiny jowl.

"Why don't you bend your head down, silly? I have to get the reins over your head!"

Everything was finally in order. Now she had only to mount. But do you think that was easy, when the stirrups were higher than her head? Natasha looked around.

There was a large stone not far from the road. She led Chubary up to it, climbed into the saddle and headed back, her cheeks flaming. The teacher was the first person she met. He had gathered up her coat, hat and galoshes and was puzzled as to how they could have got there. He had not found his glasses and squinted at Natasha with a thoughtful expression.

Natasha thought he was passing in silence because he was angry. She reined in Chubary and coughed. The teacher paid no attention.

"Well, then, give me back my galoshes," Natasha said. "Are you going home already?"

"Oh, is that you? I didn't recognise you on horseback. Where did you run off to? Chubary would have found his way home."

"That's just what I was afraid of. He would have scared everyone to death. Mamma might have thought that Yulia was killed. That's why I ran after him, to keep him from going home."

"My, aren't you clever. The idea never entered my head. So you caught him here on the road, did you?"

The teacher walked beside the horse. Natasha told him how she had fooled Chubary. He listened to her intently, gazing at the little girl's frank, open face. Finally, he threw back his head and laughed.

"Good for you! But I've lost my glasses and don't know what to do."

"Where did you lose them?"

"Somewhere over there, I think."

"I'll look for them. Here, you hold Chubary." Natasha dismounted and began walking up and down with her nose bent close to the ground.

"Here they are!" she shouted, picking up the mud-splattered glasses.

"Well, now I have a new lease of life," the teacher said in a very different voice. He wiped his glasses carefully with his handkerchief, put them on and said: "Where to now? Shall we go home or back to Yulia?"

"What's the use of going home? Please don't say anything about what happened when we get home. They'll scold Yulia for nothing and they might take Chubary away. Let's get back to Yulia. Would you like to sit behind me? No, that's not the way. You have to mount from the left side!"

The teacher, smiling at Natasha's stern commands, was about to climb up behind her. Chubary turned his head and gazed at him in wonder. He realised that this man was no rider. As soon as he raised his leg, Chubary got his chance and nipped his thigh. Finally, the teacher managed to get onto the back of the saddle. He rubbed his leg and fixed his glasses.

"You had better hold the reins. I don't know how to handle a horse," he said in some embarrassment.

Now it was Natasha's head that turned and looked at the big strange man in amazement.

Yulia's head soon mended and life continued as before. Some time later, however, she began to have headaches and the doctor said:

"It might be from that old concussion."

That winter Sonya broke her arm.

One evening she was riding home past the village watering trough.

There were several mares there, and naturally Chubary had to show off and do a dance for them on the ice. He slipped and fell.

In falling, Sonya broke her arm. The bone snapped in two places, at her wrist and a little below her elbow. As Sonya later said, "It was so painful I got an awfully sweet feeling in my mouth and then saw stars."

A man we knew was passing by. He ran over and helped Chubary and Sonya up.

"Does it hurt?"

"Yes," Sonya muttered through clenched teeth. "Ouch! Don't touch my arm! Let's go home!"

Mother and I were unravelling yarn. Suddenly, the door flew open and a cloud of steam filled the room. Then in came Sonya, holding her broken arm gingerly. Our acquaintance supported her from the other side.

Sonya's hat had fallen off, her hair was dishevelled and one eyebrow was raised nearly as high as her hairline, a habit of Mother's she copied.

"Please don't worry," she said to Mother, "I just broke my arm. But it's not Chubary's fault. He slipped and hurt himself, too."

Mother's eyes became wide with fright as she moaned: "Half my life.... You've taken half my life away with worrying about you and your Chubary.... I don't know what to do any more!"

What a commotion there was after that! Everyone rushed around, trying to be helpful. Mother tried to get Sonya's sheepskin coat off, but as soon as she touched the sleeve, Sonya screamed. Finally, she cut the sleeve off. Sonya's arm was swollen as big as a log. Someone said she should put it in hot water. This was done immediately. Then there was an argument.

"Why hot water? You're supposed to put it in cold water."

Then they made her put her arm in cold water. Sonya turned blue from pain. She held back as long as she could and then wailed:

"Oh! Oh! It hurts so badly!"

Just then Father and our plump doctor came hurrying in. The doctor bent over Sonya and threw his hands up in despair. The water disappeared immediately. Then he took a lot of bandages, little sticks and something that looked as white as chalk from his bag.

The doctor removed his jacket, rolled up his sleeves and bent over Sonya, while Mother and Father held her down.

"Ow-w-w-w-w!" Sonya screamed at the top of her voice and kicked the doctor in the stomach, sending him across the room like a rubber ball.

"Come now, dear, it'll only take a moment."

Then Sonya lost consciousness.

They put her arm in a splint, bandaged it and gave her some medicine. Then she was put to bed. But she couldn't lie still for a moment. Her arm hurt and ached so terribly that she paced up and down the room all night. I kept waking up to see her walking up and down, cradling her bandaged arm and moaning in a tearful voice:

"Ohh! Ohh! Ohh!"

Chubary was a real friend. He depended upon us just as we depended upon him.

"Chubary will never let us down," we often said.

True enough, Chubary never let us down.

Perhaps it was because he spent so much time with us and we patted and spoiled him, or perhaps it was because he was so clever. He understood us perfectly. We often spoke to him, and he was so sensitive he could guess our mood from the tone of our voice.

Once Natasha and I were sent to town on an errand. I dismounted at the market and went over to the stalls to do my shopping. Natasha rode Chubary off to the side to wait for me.

After a while I looked around and saw some men standing near them, patting Chubary and laughing.

When I had bought everything we needed we sat down in the shade, gave Chubary some clover and checked how much money I had spent. We stayed there for a while, waiting for the heat to subside before we started home.

Suddenly, I remembered that I was supposed to go to the shoemaker's. I left Natasha to guard our purchases and Chubary and hurried across town.

It was dusk by the time I returned.

Natasha said some men had come over to her again and had asked where she lived.

"I said that we lived near the lake. You should have seen their horse. It was beautiful!"

I felt a little worried about the men. Only the day before someone had said that two of our neighbour's horses had been stolen.

"Hurry, Natasha, let's start back. I don't want anything to happen to Chubary," I said.

We threw our things together in a great hurry, but it was dark by the time we had packed everything into the saddlebag and gone to the well to water Chubary.

The road followed a dark, tree-lined avenue to the ravine. There was a river on the bottom of the ravine that we had to wade across. Then we had to climb a steep hill and cross a field to the lake.

We started out along the avenue. Chubary went into his flying gallop.

Natasha sat behind me with her arms about my middle. We had no saddle.

We had only gone about two miles when I became certain that someone was following us.

"Come on, Natasha," I said, stopping Chubary and holding my bare leg up to make a step: "Get in front."

"Why?"

"We're going to go very fast and you might pull me off and fall off yourself. But if you sit in front, you can hold on to his mane."

Natasha climbed around me.

"Let's go, Chubary!"

Chubary galloped into the night. Never before had he galloped so magnificently.

A wind rose and the trees seemed to be blown backwards as we flew past.

The idea was to get to the ravine as quickly as possible, for the miller was our friend and he would never refuse to take us home.

The wind was at our backs. Each new gust brought the sound of thundering hoofs ever closer.

I realised that we could not escape our pursuers and decided upon a dangerous trick: we would hide and let them pass us.

I turned off the road and we hid beneath a branching tree.

The thundering hoofs were very close. Chubary pricked up his ears.

Suddenly, I turned cold with fear. Their horse must be a mare! That meant Chubary would certainly whinny.

"Why are we hiding?" Natasha whispered in my ear.

"Be quiet, Natasha! Don't say a word! Chubary, dear, don't you say anything, either!" I whispered anxiously, stroking his hot neck.

A shadow passed in the moonlight.

Natasha was whispering to Chubary. We were both shaking like leaves.

The mare disappeared beyond a bend in the road.

"They've gone, haven't they?"

"Wait! It's too soon to tell."

Just then Chubary raised his head, listened attentively and whinnied loudly.

We both gasped.

One, two and then three horses answered his call; several wagons appeared on the road. I thought they were heading for the lake and was overjoyed, for now we would not have to bother the miller and could ride home safely behind the wagons.

We passed the mill and the ravine and reached the fork in the road. Suddenly the wagons all turned to the left. We were alone again.

There was a full moon and the road stretched ahead of us as straight and white as a sheet.

"Come on, Chubary!"

When the last of the wagons had disappeared from view, the familiar thunder of hoofs could be heard behind us.

Natasha clutched Chubary's mane for dear life. I dug my knees into his sides and let him have his way.

A black shadow was advancing along the moonlit road. "You're our only hope, Chubary!"

Chubary started off at a gallop. Our anxiety and fear had been transferred to him. It was a mad race.

Soon the first lights of the village came into view. We flew down the street, turned a sharp corner and came to our senses in the grass in front of our gate.

Chubary had stopped so quickly that we both had flown over his head.

There was the sound of running feet. Someone with a lantern was coming towards the gate.

"Certainly, I heard them! He came galloping like mad and stopped at the gate." It was Sonya speaking.

Chubary whinnied.

"See? Did you hear that? It's Chubary. They've come back!"

"Are you sure?" Mother shouted from the porch.

"It's us! Open the gate!" I shouted in a trembling voice. "Why doesn't someone open the gate?"

We took hold of Chubary's reins and led him into the yard.

"Sweetie! Dearie! My clever boy!" Natasha was whispering.

"Natasha, don't you dare breathe a word of this to anyone!"

But we found we could not keep our adventure a secret. Sonya and Yulia went to have a look at Chubary and returned in a rage.

"What have you done to him? Go and look at him! He's dripping wet! He can't get his breath!"

"Look what you've done! You'll never get that horse again!"

"We didn't race him," Natasha answered in dismay, as she turned to look at me. "We were just riding along slowly."

"'Just riding along'! You're lying! One look at him will tell you that!"

"You're right. Natasha, why don't you tell the truth? We were going very fast. In fact, we galloped all the way!"

"Then why did you tell me not to breathe a word to anyone?"

"A word about what?" Mother asked.

"That we were running away from them," Natasha said.

The cat was out of the bag now, and so I had to tell the story from the very beginning.

We were so used to sharing everything we had with Chubary that we offered him anything we happened to be eating. Once Yulia was eating a meatball. Chubary sniffed at it with interest, so she gave him half. He ate it with pleasure and was ready for more. Another time we went for a picnic. We were ready to start back and were finishing up the odds and ends, because we didn't want to have to take any food home. We were all full, but we still had some bread and a bottle of milk left over. We gave the bread to our dog and poured the milk into Yulia's oilskin hat and offered it to Chubary as a joke.

He drank it all up and even had the appetite for a bit of bread as well.

After that the grown-ups were always amazed when we insisted that horses ate meatballs and drank milk.

"Whoever told you that?"

"Chubary. He enjoys them immensely."

We would ride into the wildest thickets, convinced that Chubary would get us back safely. Sometimes we lost our way. Then we would drop the reins and he would find the road back home.

One day we went to Mikhailovka for potatoes. The village was at the top of a steep hill. The day before it had snowed and rained. Then frost had set in and the road had turned to ice.

There were three sleighs ahead of us, but they had all stopped at the foot of the hill. The horses refused to go on. They would take several steps up the road and then turn back again.

We overtook them.

"Come on, Chubary!" We were proud to see that Chubary had obediently put his weight to the harness.

We began the climb.

After the first hundred steps we realised that we had been insanely foolish.

The water that had run down in rivulets the day before had frozen into an icy crust. Chubary kept slipping. The road was very narrow, running between the hillside and the ravine.

There was no way of turning back. We had no choice now but to go on. The people below were shouting, but we could not understand them. We watched Chubary with fear.

He stumbled onwards and fell. Then he stumbled on again, but his strength was ebbing. The end was soon in sight. People appeared at the top of the hill.

Then Chubary fell to his knees.

"Please, Chubary, please!" Sonya begged, hugging the rim of the sleigh.

Chubary crawled forward on his knees, gasping for air.

Men were running down to meet us. One grabbed the reins, another hitched on to the shafts and a third pushed the sleigh from behind.

"Heave-ho!" they all shouted. "Come on, boy! There's just a little way to go!"

We had reached the top and stood there in a daze.

"That's some horse!" people were saying. "There's

257

a horse for you! He'll never let you down! He'll get you there if he has to crawl!"

We came to our senses and turned round to Chubary gratefully.

There was a crowd around him. He had put one trembling foreleg in front of him and had dropped his exhausted, sweating head on it. His sides were heaving. I was conscience-stricken.

"Look at his breath. And it's all our fault. We're heartless, that's what we are."

Soon after that Chubary became ill.

We entered his stable one day to see him lying down. He had not touched the hay in his crib.

"Chubary, dear, what's the matter? Are you sick?"

We were very worried but decided to wait until dinner time.

There was some unpleasantness at home and when Sonya started saying something about Chubary, our parents said:

"We've no time for you now. We'll talk to you later."

Chubary lay there until evening. We covered him with a horse-blanket for the night, gave him warm water to drink and moved the hay close to him.

He drank eagerly but did not touch the hay.

That evening we held a council.

At the crack of dawn Sonya and I set out for town. We were going to call on Father's friend, who was a vet.

It was a very long walk to town.

It was bitter cold. Our faces were crimson, our eyelashes were covered with frost and the tips of our fingers were numb. But we did not notice the cold or our fatigue. We walked on in silence, listening to the monotonous scrunching of the snow underfoot, thinking of our sick Chubary.

The vet was at home. He was sitting at the table beside a samovar with a plateful of hot pancakes and sour cream in front of him. He was in excellent spirits.

"Aha, the Amazons have come!" he shouted jovially. "Sit down and have some pancakes."

"No, thank you, that's not why we've come."

We stood anxiously by the door.

The warm room gave me the shivers. Sonya's eyes and nose were shinier than the brass samovar.

"Well, I see something's wrong. Tell me all about it. Are your parents well?"

"Chubary's sick."

"No! What's wrong?"

We related all the symptoms, we said he wouldn't get up or touch his food. We also said that he was not very well to begin with, for he had been in an icy canyon and now had only one good lung.

"Well, girls, you've done the right thing by coming to me now. We may be in time. I'll be over later. You can expect me towards evening."

"Towards evening? But what if he.... You couldn't come now, could you?"

Sonya stretched her hand towards me cautiously, hoping I had a handkerchief. I looked in my pocket. There was none. She flicked a tear off her cheek.

"You've so many flies here."

The doctor looked at her and smiled.

"Come now, there's no need to cry."

Our spirits rose immediately. He would certainly come with us! Indeed, he began calling out orders:

"Give my guests some tea, dear. I'll go and find my boots and get my medicine bag."

We sat down to have some tea. The doctor kept talking and joking as he got his things together.

"Well, I'm ready now. How did you come? On horseback or in your sleigh?"

"We just came. We left very early, you know. About five o'clock. Everyone was still asleep."

"Do you mean to tell me that you walked all the way from the lake?"

"Yes."

"Well, my dear Amazons, I'm beginning to like you still more," the wonderful vet said and laughed. He and his wife exchanged glances. Then he went to hitch his horse to the carriage.

We had some tea, thanked his wife and followed him out. On the way we asked him how many horses he had cured. When we discovered that he had cured most of them, we felt better. Soon the village came into view and we were outside our gate.

The moment we reached the gate it flew open. It was Yulia and Natasha who had been running out to see if we were coming. As soon as they had caught sight of us they had pulled out the bolt and now threw open the gate for us.

We headed straight for the stable.

Chubary was still lying on his side. The vet examined him carefully. He tried to raise him, but Chubary's legs would not hold him. He fell to the ground and moaned. Natasha began to cry. We looked at the doctor with fear in our eyes.

"It's very bad. It's very bad, my dear little girls. Chubary is paralysed. There's nothing anyone can do for him now. He won't last more than two days. The best thing you can do is put him out of his misery. It will only be a second. Where's your father?"

He headed towards the house. We remained standing there over Chubary, not daring to look at each other. Finally, I raised my head. Never in all my life did I ever see such misery on everyone's face.

Towards evening Chubary got worse. He began to moan and thrash about. We huddled near him helplessly.

The next morning Sonya and I came to Father.

"Chubary's in such misery," I said, forcing the words out through the lump in my throat.

"All right," Father said. "I know. The doctor told me. Don't worry, girls, it will only take a second."

He pulled out the drawer where he kept his revolver.

We ran away and hid in a far corner of the house. We never saw Chubary again.

We stayed away till late at night, and none of the grown-ups saw the grief-stricken children walking silently out of Chubary's empty stall.

CPSIA information can be obtained
at www.ICGtesting.com
Printed in the USA
FSOW02n0926121116
27303FS

9 781589 636118